ARABIC LATTICE
lap size 46" X 59" 5 X
6 3/4 finished bl
by
Gayle Wallace

SUPPLIES: sewing machine, matt, rulers, cutter, scissors, thread, pines, extension cord/power bar, small paper bag for scraps, pillow for uncomfortable chair, iron, ironing surface, spray sizing, seam ripper.

The is quilt can be a scrap quilt or a two fabric quilt. High contrast is necessary for the design element to show up. If using scrap fabrics or going for the scrap look, I recommend that all of the lights be the same fabric.

LIGHT FABRIC 1 1/4 yds.   **DARK FABRIC 2 1/3 yds.**

BEFORE CLASS CUT:

LIGHT

7 strips 3 1/4" X 45"
4 strips 2" X 45"
5 strips 1 1/2" X 45" for first border

DARK

7 strips 3 1/4" X 45"
4 strips 2" X 45"
6 strips 5 1/2" X 45" for second border
6 strips 2 1/2" X 45" for binding

An assortment of 3 1/4" strips and
2" strips may be used if the scrap look is desired.

ARABIC LATTICE

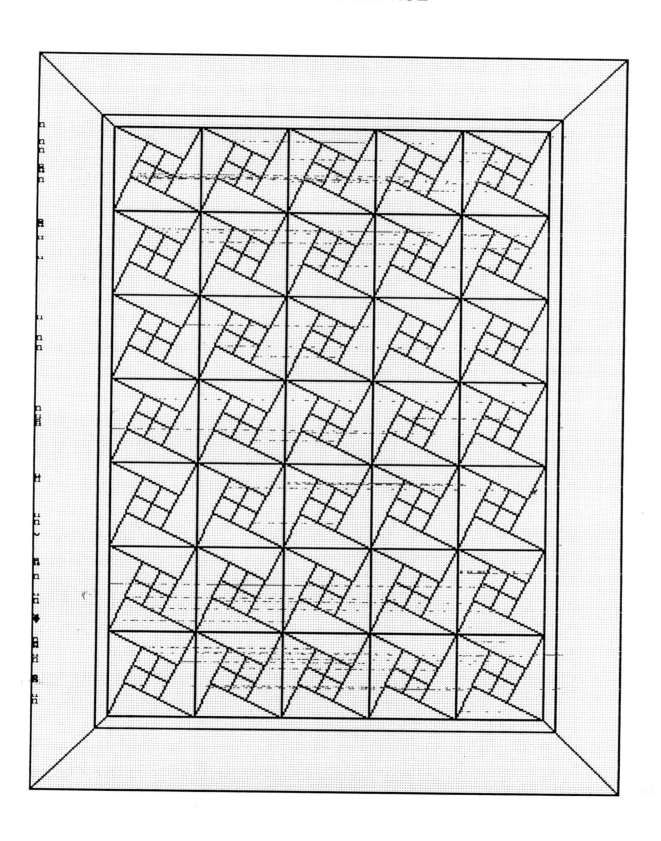

Juanita Benort 2000

VERTICAL QUILTS
with
STYLE

Bobbie A. Aug &
Sharon Newman

American Quilter's Society
P. O. Box 3290 • Paducah, KY 42002-3290

Located in Paducah, Kentucky, the American Quilter's Society (AQS) is dedicated to promoting the accomplishments of today's quilters. Through its publications and events, AQS strives to honor today's quiltmakers and their work and to inspire future creativity and innovation in quiltmaking.

EDITOR: LEE JONSSON
TECHNICAL EDITOR: BARBARA SMITH
BOOK DESIGN/ILLUSTRATIONS: ELAINE WILSON
COVER DESIGN: CHAD MURRAY
PHOTOGRAPHY: CHARLES R. LYNCH

Library of Congress Cataloging-in-Publication Data
Aug, Bobbie A.
    Vertical quilts with style / Bobbie Aug & Sharon Newman.
        p.   cm.
    ISBN 1-57432-732-1
    1. Patchwork--Patterns.   2. Quilting--Patterns.   I. Newman, Sharon,1942–II. Title.
TT835.A89 2000
746.46'041--dc21

                                                    00-029283

Additional copies of this book may be ordered from the American Quilter's Society, PO Box 3290, Paducah, KY 42002-3290

Dedication

We dedicate this book to the memory of our cherished friend Paul D. Pilgrim.

Acknowledgments

We would like to acknowledge the following individuals who have offered support and cheer: Norm Aug and Thomas Newman, Gerald E. Roy, Sandra Bennett, Jackie Reis, Gwen Oberg, Jalinda Marlar, Nancy Menard, Ann and Rex Porter, our wonderful editor Lee Jonsson, and especially Meredith Schroeder, without whom this book would not be possible. We so value her continued trust and friendship.

Contents

BICENTENNIAL BASKETS (62" x 72"), 1998, by CARLA TOCZEK.
Pattern begins on page 85.

INTRODUCTION

Vertical quilts (or bar quilts as they are commonly known) are visually dramatic and recognizable by the way they are "set" or laid out in strip fashion. In this book you will see both familiar and unusual patterns pieced into long strips that are then set between other pieced or appliquéd strips or sashing. Sometimes these quilts are referred to as strippy quilts.

According to Marston and Cunningham, "A Bars set gives your quilt many of the same elements as an alternate plain block set: room for quilting, orderliness, a balance of positive and negative space. Among old quilts set this way, we have seen tremendous variation. With many possible sizes of plain blocks between the blocks in the bars, and the width, color or print of the plain bars, the variations are endless. Therefore, it is the least standardized of sets."

The heritage of the bar set comes from quiltmakers in Durham, England, and is reflected in English and Welsh quilts. "The strip quilt and whole cloth quilt were the preferred 'canvas' on which most quilters of Wales, Durham, and Northumberland chose to work. Quilting, in their minds, was a much higher art than piecing and although they changed their ideas about color and cloth—going from white cotton to sateen and pastels in early twentieth century, they stayed true to the original format" (Rae 1987). Plain or unworked strips created an opportunity for early Durham quilters to showcase intricate, well-executed, quilting patterns.

The earliest quilts made in America were whole cloth or large pieces of cloth sewn in a medallion arrangement. The development of block patterns for patchwork started at the beginning of the nineteenth century. The basic square block was a handy size. It could be divided in a number of ways and then sewn together to form new patterns as desired. The one-patch or undivided square produced deliberate color combinations, checkerboard patterns, or concentric arrangements currently known as Trip Around the World. Set on point, the square created the simplest bar quilt. Dividing a block into quarters vertically and horizontally produced the four-patch. Dividing a

A BARS SET GIVES YOUR QUILT MANY OF THE SAME ELEMENTS AS AN ALTERNATE PLAIN BLOCK SET: ROOM FOR QUILTING, ORDERLINESS, A BALANCE OF POSITIVE AND NEGATIVE SPACE.

YOU WILL FIND BAR QUILTS IN EVERY DECADE OF AMERICAN QUILTMAKING.

block into quarters diagonally gave much more versatility to the design, yet retained simple piecing units. Other divisions included nine, sixteen, twenty-five, and forty-nine squares (von Gwinner 1988).

You will find bar quilts in every decade of American quiltmaking. The most recognized bar quilts were made by the Amish and were made from strips of wool challis, wool crepe, silk crepe, or cotton, with the texture of the quilting stitches enriching the plain fabrics.

Many early-American chintz quilts were sewn in bar sets. The printed chintz designs did not showcase the quilting as plain cloth would have, but resulted in very beautiful quilts. These early quilts included one-patch, four-patch, and nine-patch blocks—easy patterns for any quiltmaker.

Baskets and stars were also popular patterns found in old bar quilts. Baby Blocks, Roman Coins, Zigzag, Flying Geese, and Stacked Bricks were allover patterns set in bars. Sometimes redwork embroidery was used in the sashing strips. Although there were many more patchwork bar quilts than appliqué bar quilts, some of the appliqué patterns used in the alternating strips included Morning Glory, Magic Vine, and Roses. Many Mennonite quilts from Pennsylvania had a bar-set design on the front and a backing with pieced bars, as well.

Among the bar quilts are notable variations, which still visually convey the vertical bars. Gwen Marston and Joe Cunningham mention one such variation in their book *Sets and Borders*, "Even more rare is the Streak of Lightning set which we classify as a Bars variation. Unlike the regular Bars set, it has no plain strips—it has plain triangles instead. By starting every other column of blocks with a half-block you make the triangles overlap to form zigzags." These quilts composed of even the plainest fabrics and constructed of one simple pattern piece are exciting and visually complex.

Today, bars can be made from solid or print fabric, and they can be narrow or wide. Bars can also be made from two or more vertical strips sewn together lengthwise, which are then alternated with patchwork strips.

Any block pattern that can be sewn can be set in bars. The blocks can be placed in strips set straight or turned on point. Even a sampler of patterns can be set in this manner.

While not all bar quilts are set vertically, the number is greater than those set horizontally. One reason may be that we are accustomed to seeing many familiar objects such as trees, flowers, plants, and people on a vertical plane, and our eyes seem to prefer an "up and down" direction.

We have had so much fun making bar quilts. The fact that only about half of the quilt top needs to be pieced or appliquéd means you get to the setting stage much faster. And in general, cutting the fabric for a bar quilt is very economical and the piecing is easier. We're sure that once you have made a quilt using a vertical set, you'll be hooked, too!

TODAY, BARS CAN BE MADE FROM SOLID OR PRINT FABRIC, AND THEY CAN BE NARROW OR WIDE.

SINGLE ELEGANCE (76" x 88"), PIECED BY SHARON
NEWMAN, QUILTED BY TARA WALES, 1998. The richness of the
1830 reproduction fabrics produces an exciting quilt with a very simple
pattern. Squares finished 4¾" are set on point with a "float," creating a
7½"-wide sashing. Only two rows of patchwork are set symmetrically
with the same size bars of red and gold prints. The quilting is a grid-
and-pumpkin seed design quilted in the pattern on the reverse side of
the quilt. The edge is finished with two-sided binding. (See binding
directions, page 19.) From the collection of Sharon Newman.

General Instructions

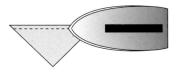

Press seam to set it.

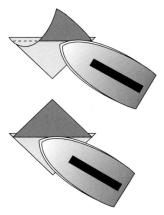

Use iron to push top triangle back.

FIGURE 1. Press instead of iron.

Read through the following information before you begin your quilting project.

BEGINNING BASICS

- Wash and press the fabric before measuring and cutting.
- Remove selvages from the fabric.
- Use a ¼" seam allowance throughout. Sew 10 to 12 stitches per inch.
- Be as accurate as possible in your measuring, cutting, and sewing. A .5 mechanical pencil will help you keep your pencil lines consistent. The 6" x 24" acrylic rulers are helpful when cutting the long sashing strips and borders.
- Generally, press seam allowances toward the darker fabric with the iron on the "cotton" setting. We prefer steam, but use caution when pressing bias edges. Place your patchwork dark side up on your ironing board. Press the seam first to set it and also to flatten any puckers in the stitching. Gently lift the dark fabric and let the iron push it back over the seam allowance (Fig. 1). Do not pull on the fabric, which could cause stretching. Notice that we are using the iron in a careful way—pressing, not ironing.

CHOOSING FABRICS FOR BAR QUILTS

The sashing fabric you choose for a bar quilt will have a greater impact than the sashing fabric you choose for a traditional, repetitive-block quilt. Fabrics that work well in bar quilts include florals, solids, or printed stripes. You may combine any of these selections for a pieced sashing as well.

The selection of colors and designs in striped or border prints makes it easy to coordinate these fabrics with the stash of prints used for the pieced or appliquéd panels. When you have selected a printed stripe, determine whether it is printed symmetrically. If it is not, you can still get the look of symmetry by cutting and rotating the design. Any width of stripe can be cut. Narrow stripes can be framed by solids or prints. Check the fabric to ensure there are enough repeats for the size of quilt you have planned. Many stripes are printed with four or more repeats across the width of the fabric. Different stripes can also be combined in one bar quilt. (See Seven Rows of Scraps, page 55.)

Choose colors for bar quilts as you would for any quilt. Pick the colors you enjoy sewing. Bar quilts allow you to use a lot of different fabrics, and you may choose a family of colors that work together such as fall colors, festive colors, patriotic colors, or bright colors—the combinations are limitless.

ARRANGING BLOCKS IN BAR SETTINGS

It is easy to get your quilt to lay flat if you take a few simple measurements. Mark with pins the pieced panels and long sashing strips at the half and quarter points (Fig. 2). Place the pieced panel and sashing strip right sides together, matching the center and quarter pins and the ends of the strips. Pin the length of the strips together.

Some patterns will piece together easier and look better if they are aligned not just vertically, but also horizontally. Specific measurements have been noted in patterns where having this interval would be helpful (Fig. 3).

SETTING BLOCKS ON POINT

Many vertical set quilts feature pieced blocks set on point. Simple blocks, such as Four Patch, Nine Patch, and Variable Star, are often used. This arrangement of blocks requires the use of setting triangles. Use the chart, shown on page 14, when you need to know the diagonal measurement of a block. Remember, the diagonal measurement of a square is 1.414 times the side of the square. We've shown both the actual decimal measurement as well as the most practical fractional equivalent.

SIDE AND CORNER TRIANGLES

Use the chart, shown on page 15, to determine the sizes of side and corner triangles needed to set blocks on point. Remember, the size of the square to cut for the corner triangles is half the diagonal measurement of the adjacent finished block plus ⅞". Cut two squares once diagonally to get four corners. The size of the square to cut for the side triangles is the diagonal measurement of the adjacent finished block plus 1¼". Cut one square twice diagonally to get four side triangles (Fig. 4).

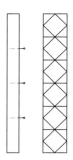

FIGURE 2. Mark sashing at half and quarter measurements.

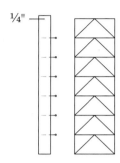

FIGURE 3. Mark sashing strips at measurements given in patterns. Allow for ¼" seam allowance at the top of sashing strips.

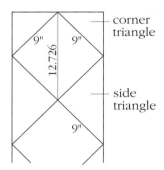

Corner Triangles
The diagonal of a 9" block is 12.726 (table, p. 14).
12.726 ÷ 2 = 6.363 + .875 (⅞") = 7.238 or 7¼"

7¼"

Side Triangles
The diagonal of a 9" block is 12.726.
12.726 + 1.25 = 13.976 or 14"

14"

FIGURE 4. Determine square size to cut for making corner and side triangles.

SETTING BLOCKS ON POINT

Diagonal Measurement

SIZE OF BLOCK	DECIMAL	NEAREST FRACTION
1	1.414	1½
1½	2.121	2⅛
2	2.828	2⅞
2½	3.535	3⅝
3	4.242	4¼
3½	4.949	5
4	5.656	5⅝
4½	6.363	6⅜
5	7.070	7⅛
5½	7.777	7⅞
6	8.484	8½
6½	9.191	9¼
7	9.898	10
7½	10.605	10⅝
8	11.312	11⅜
8½	12.019	12⅛
9	12.726	12¾
9½	13.433	12½
10	14.140	14¼
10½	14.847	14⅞
11	15.554	15⅝
11½	16.261	16⅜
12	16.968	17
12½	17.675	17¾
13	18.382	18½
13½	19.089	19⅛
14	19.796	19⅞
14½	20.503	20½
15	21.210	21¼
15½	21.917	22
16	22.624	22⅝

(All measurements are in inches.)

SIDE AND CORNER TRIANGLES

Finished Block Size	Square Size to Cut for Corner Triangles ▱		Square Size to Cut for Side Triangles ▨	
	DECIMAL	NEAREST FRACTION	DECIMAL	NEAREST FRACTION
1	1.582	1⅝	2.664	2¾
1½	1.935	2	3.371	3⅜
2	2.289	2⅜	4.078	4⅛
2½	2.75	2¾	4.785	4⅞
3	2.996	3	5.492	5½
3½	3.349	3⅜	6.199	6¼
4	3.703	3¾	6.906	7
4½	4.056	4⅛	7.613	7⅝
5	4.410	4½	8.320	8⅜
5½	4.763	4⅞	9.027	9⅛
6	5.117	5⅛	9.734	9¾
6½	5.471	5½	10.441	10½
7	5.824	5⅞	11.148	11¼
7½	6.200	6¼	11.900	12
8	6.531	6⅝	12.571	12⅝
8½	6.884	6⅞	13.269	13⅜
9	7.238	7¼	13.976	14
9½	7.592	7⅝	14.683	14¾
10	7.945	8	15.390	15½
10½	8.299	8⅜	16.097	16⅛
11	8.75	8¾	16.804	16⅞
11½	9.006	9⅛	17.5	17½
12	9.359	9⅜	18.218	18¼
12½	9.713	9¾	18.925	19
13	10.066	10⅛	19.632	19¾
13½	10.420	10½	20.339	20⅜
14	10.773	10⅞	21.046	21⅛
14½	11.127	11⅛	21.753	21¾
15	11.480	11½	22.460	22½
15½	11.834	11⅞	23.167	23¼
16	12.187	12¼	23.874	23⅞

(All measurements are in inches.)

QUILT BORDERS

ADDING BORDERS WITH STRAIGHT CORNERS

Lay the quilt top on a flat surface and use a plastic or metal tape measure to determine the length of the quilt through the center and each side of the quilt top. The two outer measurements should be the same as the center measurement. The two border strips should be cut to match the measured length.

Fold the quilt top in half and mark the center of each side of the quilt with pins. Fold in half again and mark the fourths, then fold again and mark the eighths. Fold and mark the centers, quarters, and eighths of the border strips in the same fashion.

Match the pins as you pin the side borders to the quilt top. As you stitch each border, add more pins between the divisions as necessary to ensure that no stretching takes place. Sew with the border strips on top, as they are more stable than the pieced quilt top. Ease in any fullness, if necessary. Press.

To add the top and bottom borders, measure the width of the quilt top through the center and across the top and bottom, including the side borders. Cut border strips to this measurement. Attach the border strips to the quilt top and bottom edges, using the same method as described above.

Add additional borders, if desired, using the same technique. Always complete one border before adding another.

FIGURE 5. Measure length and width through the middle and on each side.

ADDING BORDERS WITH MITERED CORNERS

Lay the quilt top on a flat surface and use a plastic or metal tape measure to determine the length of the quilt top through the center and each side of the quilt top (Fig. 5). The two outer measurements should be the same as the center measurement. The two border strips should be cut to the measured length plus two finished border widths, plus seam allowances, plus two to three inches for extra mitering length.

Fold the quilt top in half and mark the center of each side with pins. Fold in half again and mark the fourths, then fold again and mark the eighths. Fold and mark the centers of the border strips. Measure the quarter marks and eighth marks on the quilt top and transfer these measurements to the border strips and mark with pins (Fig. 6).

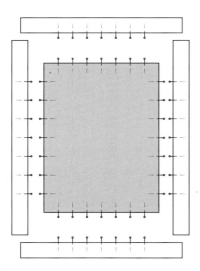

FIGURE 6. Measure and match the center, fourths, and eighths.

Pin each border strip to the quilt top, matching center, quarter, and eighth marks. Start and end your stitching ¼" from the corners of the quilt. Sew the four borders to the quilt top, backstitching at each starting and stopping point (Fig. 7).

As you sew each border, add more pins between the divisions as necessary to ensure that no stretching takes place. Sew with the border strips on top, as they are more stable than the pieced quilt top. Ease in any fullness, if necessary. Press. Add more borders to the quilt as desired, leaving all the ends unfinished.

Once you have added the borders, you are ready to miter the corners. Place one corner of the quilt on your work surface, right side up. Fold the corner, right sides together, aligning the side edge with the top edge exactly. Begin stitching at the end of the sewing line ¼" from the corner, following the angle of the fold, to the edge of the outer border (Fig. 8).

Turn to the right side, open the corner, and press. Trim seam allowance to ¼" (Fig. 9). Repeat miter instructions for remaining corners.

PREPARING THE QUILT FOR QUILTING

PLANNING THE QUILTING DESIGN

Whether you plan to machine or hand quilt your project may influence your choice of quilting designs. Diagonal lines, grids, and parallel lines are popular background patterns. Mark the fabric with a pencil and ruler, or use masking tape as a guide. Free-motion machine stippling is another popular background design. Fancier patterns, such as wreaths, feathers, cables, and baskets, work well in open spaces like alternate blocks, side triangles, corner triangles, and border areas. These are usually combined with background quilting. Many of these designs are available in commercial stencils and pattern books. However, it can be fun to use personalized motifs and symbols in an original design. You may wish to incorporate designs that fit in the space desired without overlapping the seam allowances. It is also a good idea to include your name and the date the quilt was completed in your quilting lines.

The quantity of quilting you plan for your quilt should be adequate to hold the batting in place and should be

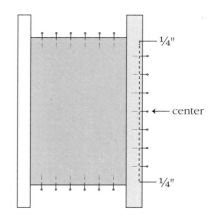

FIGURE 7. Sew borders, starting and stopping ¼" from the corners of the quilt top.

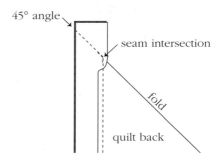

FIGURE 8. With right sides together, sew from the seam intersection to the corner.

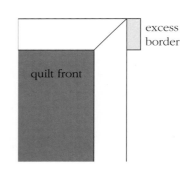

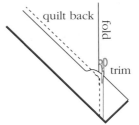

FIGURE 9. After checking the miter on the front of the quilt, trim the excess border, leaving a ¼" seam allowance.

evenly distributed over the entire quilt. Whichever designs you choose, plan them out on the quilt's surface before you begin marking.

MARKING THE QUILTING DESIGN

Thoroughly press the quilt top, making sure all seam allowances lie flat. Test the pencil or marker you have chosen on a scrap of your quilt fabric to make sure you can remove the marks later. If it is necessary for you to use more than one type of marker, test them all before proceeding. Use a gentle hand when marking.

A non-skid type of surface, such as a rotary cutting mat, is great to use under your quilt top when marking, as this eliminates "drag" and fabric slippage. Begin marking wherever you like. However, borders should be marked from the corners to the center of each side to allow for any adjustments needed in border pattern repeat. Mark all the quilting lines on the entire quilt top.

CHOOSING BATTING

Choose the batting thickness and fiber content according to the appearance desired for your finished quilt. Batting comes in a variety of fibers including cotton, polyester, cotton and polyester blends, silk, and wool. Some are easier to quilt through than others. Many quilt guilds have conducted comparison tests on different types of batting in order to make recommendations to their members. The most important factor in choosing a batting is the quality of the product. Take time to choose the right one for your quilt. Read the label on the one you choose, as some battings require prewashing or other preparation before being layered into the quilt.

Purchase a batting size at least 4 inches longer and 4 inches wider than your finished quilt top.

LAYERING THE QUILT TOP, BATTING, AND BACKING

Measure the width and length of the quilt top through the centers. Cut and assemble the backing so that it extends at least 2 inches beyond the quilt top on all four sides. Press seam allowances open. Note: All quilt backings in this book are seamed vertically unless otherwise noted.

Lay the backing fabric on a smooth, flat surface wrong side up. Pull the edges of the backing taught to eliminate any fullness or wrinkles. Tape or pin at corners and intervals along the edge to maintain tautness. Keep edges as straight as possible and corners square. Spread the batting over the backing and trim the batting to match the backing. Center the quilt top on the batting and backing. Starting at the center of the quilt, pin all three layers together with 1" safety pins. Working out from the center, pin about every eight inches (Fig. 10).

After the quilt has been pin basted, release the tape or pins at the edge of the backing and fold the backing over the batting and pin to seal the edges (Fig. 11).

Begin quilting in the center of the quilt. Continue to enlarge the quilted area from the center out. Work to make your stitches even, not just small.

BINDING THE QUILT

All binding yardages are for 2"-wide strips, which can be straight-grain or bias. The following special techniques were used for binding some of the quilts.

TWO-SIDED BINDING

(See SINGLE ELEGANCE on page 10 for an example.)

- Measure the perimeter of your quilt and add about 10" for ease in mitering the corners.
- From the two fabrics chosen for the binding, cut the back binding strips 1½" wide by the length determined. Cut the front binding strips 1" wide by the length determined.
- Press the back binding strip in half lengthwise, wrong sides together, creating a ¾"-wide folded strip.
- Using a ¼" seam allowance, sew the raw edges of the folded strip to the right side of the unfolded front binding strip (Fig. 12, page 20).
- To apply the binding to the quilt, trim the batting and backing even with the raw edges of the quilt top. Place the front strip on the edge of the quilt, right sides together. Sew with a ¼" seam allowance (Fig. 13, page 20). Miter the corners and finish the ends.

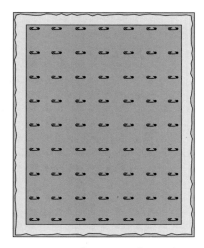

FIGURE 10. Working out from the center, pin about every 8".

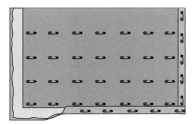

FIGURE 11. Fold the backing over the batting and pin to protect the edges.

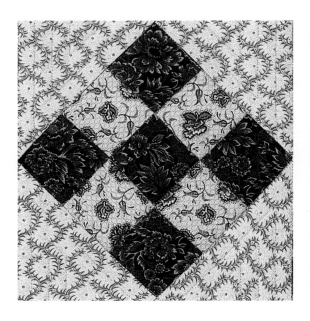

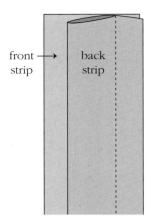

FIGURE 12. Sew folded strip to right side of front strip.

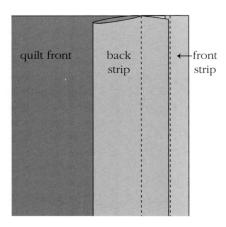

FIGURE 13. Sew the front strip to the quilt, right sides together.

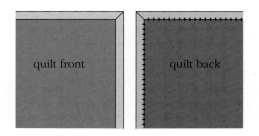

FIGURE 14. Finished two-sided binding.

• Fold the two-sided binding along the seam between the front and back strips. Hand stitch on the back of the quilt to cover the seam line (Fig. 14).

FRENCH BINDING

(See STAIRWAY TO HEAVEN on page 51, for an example.)

• This technique requires a separate binding strip for each side of the quilt. To determine each strip's length, measure the sides of your quilt and add about an inch at each end for ease in finishing the corners.

• Cut straight or bias strips 2¾" wide by the lengths determined.

• Fold strips and press wrong sides together, matching raw edges.

• Place the raw edge of the binding on the trimmed edge of the quilt top and sew with a ¼" seam allowance. Repeat on the opposite side of the quilt.

• Pull all of the binding to the back of the quilt. Press to keep the edge smooth. Sew the binding in place. No binding is left showing on the front (Fig. 15).

• Sew binding strips to the remaining two sides of the quilt, overlapping the binding already sewn in place. Pull completely to the back again.

• Trim out the bulk at the corners, fold ends even with the quilt edge, and stitch binding in place (Fig. 16).

SIGNING YOUR QUILT

Signing a quilt can be as simple as writing your name with a permanent-ink fabric pen. It can be as involved as an elaborate cross-stitch project embellished with embroidery. As suggested earlier, it is a good idea to quilt your name and the date in the quilting design.

Include on your label, or on the quilt itself, your name as the quiltmaker (add your maiden name—it will be forgotten otherwise), the date the quilt was finished, and the city and state where you live. Use the label to tell the story of the quilt. What is the pattern? Was it made as a gift? Give as much information as possible.

Iron a square of muslin on a piece of freezer paper to stabilize the fabric for ease in writing. Use a permanent

VERTICAL QUILTS WITH STYLE – BOBBIE AUG & SHARON NEWMAN

fine-point pen and write slowly. Be sure to remove the paper before stitching the label onto the back of the quilt.

Press under a ¼" seam allowance on the top and one adjoining side of the label. Position label on lower corner of quilt back so that the two unpressed sides of the label will be caught in the seam when the binding is attached. This not only saves you some sewing, but also provides extra assurance that the label will remain in place. Hand stitch the folded edges to the quilt backing.

ATTACHING A SLEEVE

Prepare and sew a sleeve for hanging your quilt at the same time the quilt is made. Using a portion of the backing fabric makes the sleeve unobtrusive, but any fabric may be used.

Cut a 9"-wide strip the width of the quilt, less 2". On each end, turn under ¼", then turn under another ¼". Stitch to hem both ends. Fold the fabric in half lengthwise with wrong sides together. Align the raw edges of the sleeve with the top edge of the quilt prior to attaching the binding. When the binding is attached, the sleeve seam will be included in the binding seam. Using a large running stitch, hand sew the lower edge of the sleeve through the backing and batting, taking a stitch through to the front of the quilt about every 1½". If matching thread or a neutral color is used, the stitches on the front will not be visible when the quilt is displayed. This enables the entire quilt to support the weight of the quilt while hanging.

A hanging sleeve can also be added to a finished/bound quilt. Cut a 9"-wide strip the width of the quilt, less 2". On each end, turn under ¼", then turn under another ¼". Stitch to hem both ends. Fold the fabric in half lengthwise with wrong sides together and stitch a ¼" seam, forming a tube. Press the seam open and center seam on the back of the tube. Press. Align the sleeve ½" below the binding along the top of the quilt. Using a large running stitch, hand sew the sleeve to the quilt through the backing and batting, taking a stitch through to the front of the quilt about every 1½".

FIGURE 15. Pull all of the binding to the back of quilt. No binding shows on the front.

FIGURE 16. Repeat for the top and bottom binding strips.

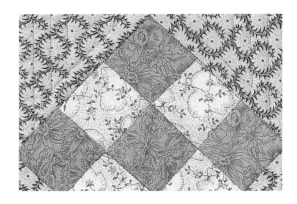

MENNONITE NINE PATCH (70" x 76"). The 6½" Nine-Patch blocks (c. 1880) are set on point with a double-pink background. The 7"-wide sashing strips are a black, green, and yellow print. The quilt backing is pieced using the green print and gold print from the Nine-Patch blocks on the front. The sashing strips are quilted with a feather design. The patchwork blocks are quilted ½" away from the seams, with the double-pink background quilted in straight lines 1" apart, echoing the angle. From the collection of Sharon Newman.

Vertical Quilts with Style – Bobbie Aug & Sharon Newman

Patterns
for
Vertical Set
Quilts

VERTICAL QUILTS WITH STYLE – BOBBIE AUG & SHARON NEWMAN

Using Squares

White Diamonds

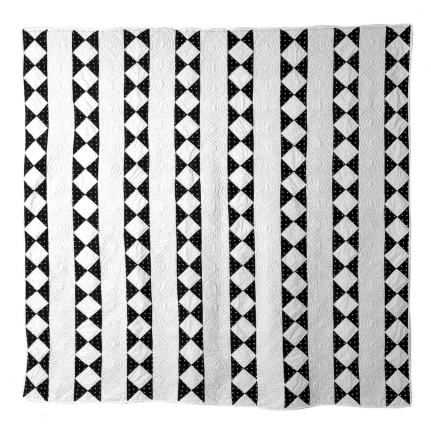

WHITE DIAMONDS (82" x 79"), QUILTER UNKNOWN, c. 1920, TOP FINISHED BY CAROLINE PETERSON, ATWOOD, KANSAS, AND DOROTHY VICE, BEAVER CITY, NEBRASKA. Indigo blue print and white quilts were popular in the first quarter and the last quarter of the nineteenth century. It is unusual to find one made in the twentieth century. So, when Bobbie found this quilt top at an antique booth at the 1998 AQS Quilt Show in Paducah, Kentucky, she didn't hesitate in making the purchase.

QUILT SIZE 80½" x 82"

Note: The 1920s quilt in the photo is wider than it is long, and it is pieced in traditional strippy style with no top and bottom borders. Because of the accuracy of today's rotary cutting and machine sewing, the following pattern instructions will produce a quilt that is longer than it is wide. If you would like an even larger quilt, you can add panels to make it wider or add two or three more units to each pieced panel to make it longer. Be sure to add extra length to each sashing strip for the longer quilt.

FABRIC REQUIREMENTS

SASHING, PIECED STRIPS, AND BINDING:
  5 yards white solid

TRIANGLES:
  2⅝ yards blue with white polka dots

BACKING:
  5⅜ yards white solid

CUTTING LIST

WHITE SOLID:
    7 sashing strips 5¾" x 82½"
  128 squares 4⅜" x 4⅜"

BLUE WITH WHITE POLKA DOTS:
  60 squares 6¾" x 6¾", cut twice diagonally

White Diamonds

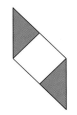

FIGURE 1. Unit A, make 112.

FIGURE 2. Unit B, make 8.

FIGURE 3. Unit C, make 8.

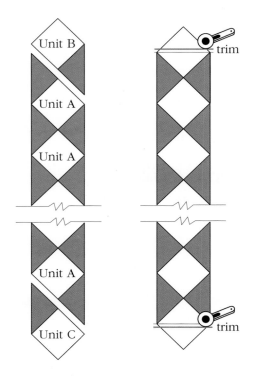

FIGURE 4.   **FIGURE 5.**

SEWING DIRECTIONS

PIECING THE PANELS

✦ Sew two blue triangles to opposite sides of a white square, keeping the long side of the blue triangles to the outside of the panel to form a diagonal row, Unit A, Fig. 1. Press.

✦ Sew one triangle to the lower right side of a white square to form Unit B, Fig. 2. Press.

✦ In the same manner, sew one triangle to the upper left side of a white square to form Unit C, Fig. 3. Press.

✦ Arrange 14 of Unit A so that the white squares are on point and in a straight vertical line. Stitch the units together to form a panel. Press. You will need eight pieced panels (Fig. 4).

✦ Sew one Unit B to the top of each panel. Press.

✦ Sew one Unit C to the bottom of each panel. Press.

ASSEMBLING THE QUILT TOP

✦ Mark the pieced panels and sashing strips ¼" from the edge at each corner and at the half and quarter points.

✦ Arrange the panels and sashing strips as seen in the photo, beginning and ending with a pieced panel. Pin and sew the pieced panels and sashing strips, matching marked points. Press. Note: The top and bottom edges will be irregularly shaped.

✦ Trim the square at the top and bottom of each pieced panel even with the edge of the sashing strips (Fig. 5).

FINISHING THE QUILT

✦ Mark the quilting design. The design for this quilt is a triple cable in the white sashing strips. Each triangle and white square is outline stitched ¼" inside the seam lines.

✦ Layer quilt top, batting, and backing, and baste.

✦ Quilt and bind.

✦ Sign and date your quilt.

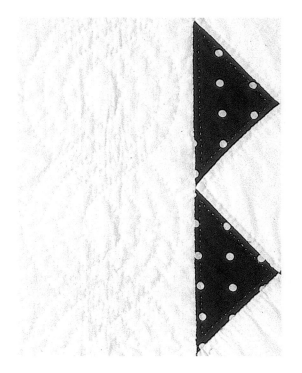

QUILTING DESIGN

VERTICAL QUILTS WITH STYLE – BOBBIE AUG & SHARON NEWMAN

Aztec Gold

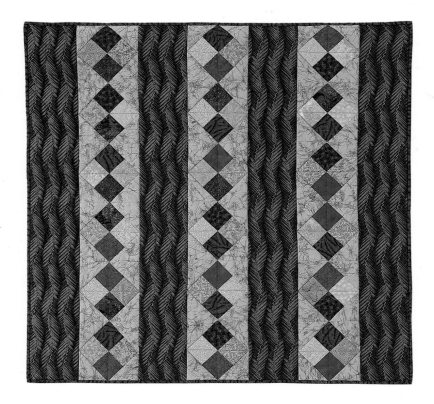

AZTEC GOLD (35" x 34¼"), MADE BY GWEN OBERG, ALBUQUERQUE, NEW MEXICO, 1998. When we asked Gwen to construct a bar set quilt using a Four-Patch on point, we knew it would be wonderful because Gwen uses exciting colors with a New Mexican influence. We weren't disappointed!

QUILT SIZE 39" x 34"

FABRIC REQUIREMENTS

SASHING:

1 yard blue print

BLOCKS:

6 fat eighths of assorted red prints

6 fat eighths of assorted gold prints

BACKGROUND:

⅔ yard blue background print

BACKING:

1 yard

BINDING:

¼ yard for ¼" (finished width) straight-grain binding

CUTTING LIST

SASHING:

4 strips 6" x 34½"

ASSORTED RED PRINTS:

6 strips 2½" x 20½" (one strip from each red print)

ASSORTED GOLD PRINTS:

6 strips 2½" x 20½" (one strip from each gold print)

BACKGROUND PRINT:

36 squares 3¾" x 3¾", cut once diagonally

BINDING:

4 strips 2" x 44"

Aztec Gold

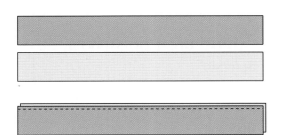

FIGURE 1. Make six paired strips.

FIGURE 2. Cut strips into 2½" segments.

FIGURE 3. Make 18 four-patches.

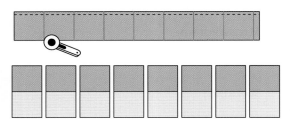

FIGURE 4. Add corners to four-patches.

SEWING DIRECTIONS

PIECING THE FOUR-PATCHES

✦ With right sides together, sew a red strip and a gold strip together lengthwise. Make six paired strips (Fig. 1). Press seam allowances toward the red.

✦ Cut the pieced strips into 2½" segments. Cut 36 segments (Fig. 2).

✦ Sew two segments together as shown to make a four-patch unit. Make 18 four-patches (Fig. 3).

PIECING THE PANELS

✦ Sew a triangle of background fabric to opposite sides of a Four-Patch block. Press. Sew triangles to remaining sides. Press. Stitch triangles to remaining Four-Patch blocks in the same manner (Fig. 4).

✦ With the red squares in vertical alignment, arrange and piece three rows of six blocks (Fig. 5).

ASSEMBLING THE QUILT TOP

✦ Mark sashing strips ¼" from the edge at each corner and at 5⅝" intervals.

✦ Arrange the panels and sashing strips, beginning and ending with a sashing strip. Pin and sew the pieced panels and sashing strips, matching marked points with seams. Press.

FINISHING THE QUILT

✦ Mark the quilting design. In addition to quilting in the seam of each sashing strip, Gwen quilted a vertical and horizontal line through each Four-Patch and a large diamond cable in the sashing strips.

✦ Layer quilt top, batting, and backing, and baste.

✦ Quilt and bind.

✦ Sign and date your quilt.

FIGURE 5. Piece three rows of six blocks.

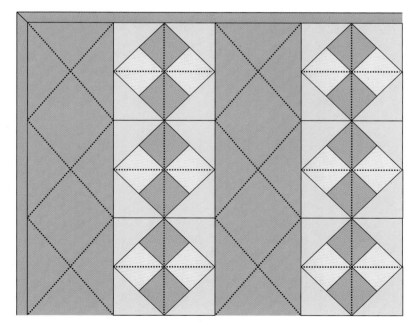

QUILTING DESIGN

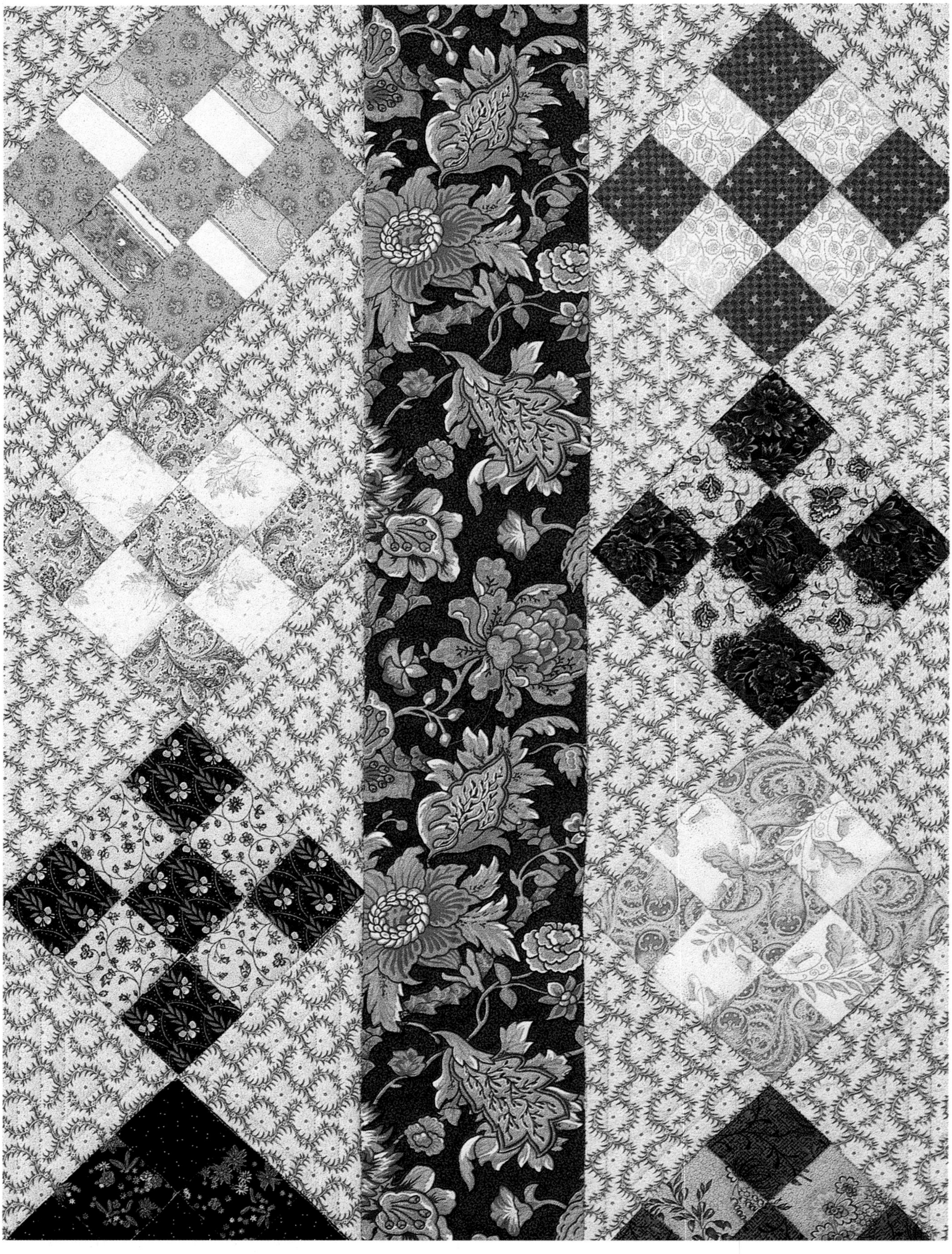

Nine-Patch Bars

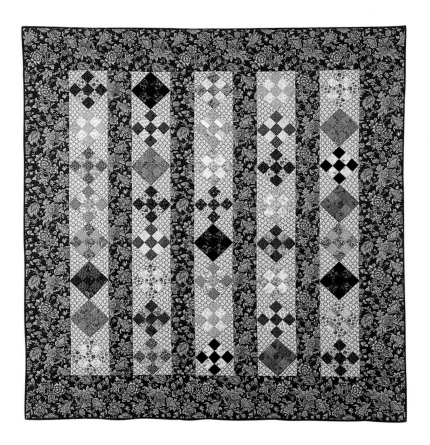

QUILT SIZE 82½" x 96½"

Note: The following project instructions are for a quilt with five rows of nine Nine Patches, not five rows of eight Nine Patches as shown in the photo.

FABRIC REQUIREMENTS

BORDER AND SASHING STRIPS:

4¾ yards blue floral

BACKGROUND TRIANGLES:

2 yards light blue print

BLOCKS:

2½ yards assorted prints

BACKING:

6 yards

BINDING:

¾ yard

NINE-PATCH BARS (81½" x 94¼"), MADE BY BOBBIE AUG, 1998. There's an old saying that little girls were to have pieced a Nine-Patch quilt top by the age of nine. True or not, this pattern has been popular with quiltmakers for over a century. Perhaps quilters have been attracted to this design because of its simplicity. However, when rich fabrics are used and the blocks are set on point, the Nine-Patch can hold its own with any other pattern.

CUTTING LIST

BLUE FLORAL PRINT:

2 strips 10" x 83" for top and bottom borders

2 strips 10" x 77" for side borders

4 strips 5½" x 77" for sashing

LIGHT BLUE PRINT:

10 squares 5⅛" x 5⅛", cut once diagonally for corner triangles

20 squares 9¾" x 9¾", cut twice diagonally for side triangles

ASSORTED PRINTS:

2½" strips x width of fabric (22" or 44")

4 strips 2" x 44

Nine-Patch Bars

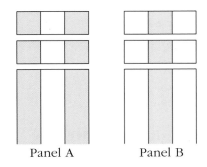

Panel A   Panel B

FIGURE 1. Cut 2½" segments.

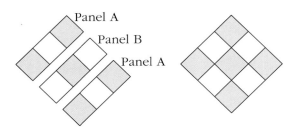

Panel A
Panel B
Panel A

FIGURE 2. Assemble Nine-Patch blocks.

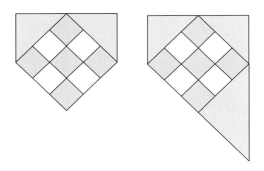

FIGURE 3. Add corner triangles to top and bottom blocks. Add a side triangle to the lower right side of top blocks.

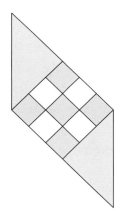

FIGURE 4. Add side triangles to opposite sides of the remaining blocks.

SEWING DIRECTIONS

PIECING THE NINE PATCHES

✦ Using two contrasting fabrics, make two panels with a dark strip sewn lengthwise to each side of a light strip.

✦ Using the same contrasting fabrics, make one panel with a light strip sewn lengthwise to each side of a dark strip.

✦ Cut each pieced strip into 2½" segments (Fig. 1).

✦ Assemble the Nine Patches as shown, using two segments from Panel A and one segment from Panel B (Fig. 2).

✦ Make 45 Nine-Patch blocks using the assorted prints.

PIECING THE PANELS

✦ Arrange five rows of nine blocks set on point.

✦ For each of the five vertical rows, add corner triangles to adjacent sides of each top and bottom block. Press (Fig. 3).

✦ Add a side triangle to the lower right side of the top block and the upper left side of the bottom block as shown. Press.

✦ Add two side triangles to opposite sides of the remaining 35 Nine-Patch blocks as shown (Fig. 4). Press.

✦ Sew the nine units (seven center units and two end units) together for each of the five vertical rows, matching seams (Fig. 5).

   VERTICAL QUILTS WITH STYLE – BOBBIE AUG & SHARON NEWMAN

ASSEMBLING THE QUILT TOP

✦ Mark sashing strips ¼" from the edge at each corner at 4¼" for first and last blocks with 8½" intervals for remainder of blocks.

✦ Arrange the panels and sashing strips, beginning and ending with a pieced panel. Pin and sew the pieced panels and sashing strips, matching marked points with the seams. Press.

✦ Sew the side borders to the quilt top as described in Adding Borders with Straight Corners, page 16. Press.

✦ Sew the top and bottom border to the quilt top as described.

FINISHING THE QUILT

✦ Mark the quilting design. The design for this quilt is four vertical lines, 1" apart in the sashing; a plus, an X, and a box in the Nine-Patches; touching hearts in the large background triangles with half-hearts touching in small top and bottom triangles; and straight parallel lines, 2" apart and perpendicular to the edge of the quilt in the outside border.

✦ Layer quilt top, batting, and backing, and baste.

✦ Quilt and bind.

✦ Sign and date your quilt.

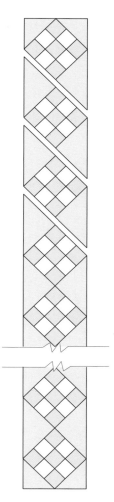

FIGURE 5. Make 5 vertical rows.

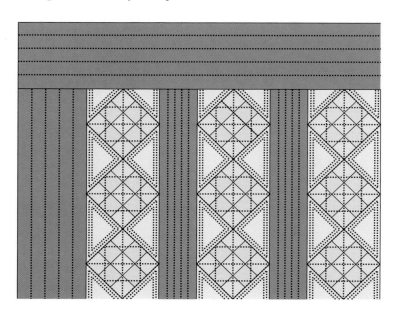

QUILTING DESIGN

VERTICAL QUILTS WITH STYLE — BOBBIE AUG & SHARON NEWMAN

Garden Path

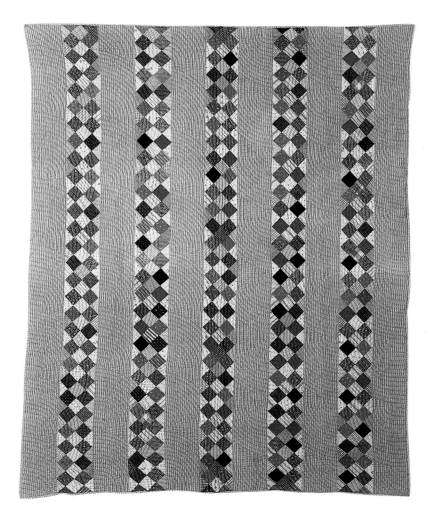

GARDEN PATH (72" x 85½"), QUILTER UNKNOWN, C. 1900. Sharon purchased this quilt from an antique dealer in Ft. Worth, Texas, in 1997. The pattern was published during the 1930s.

QUILT SIZE 69" x 84"

FABRIC REQUIREMENTS

SASHING:

2¾ yards pink

PATCHWORK:

2½ yards assorted fabrics

SETTING TRIANGLES:

2 yards assorted light fabrics

BACKING:

5½ yards

BINDING:

¾ yard

CUTTING LIST

PINK SASHING:

6 strips 7" x 85½"

ASSORTED FABRICS FOR PATCHWORK:

410 squares 2¾" x 2¾"

 5 squares 4⅜" x 4⅜", cut twice diagonally

ASSORTED LIGHT PRINTS FOR SETTING TRIANGLES:

 70 squares 4⅜" x 4⅜", cut twice diagonally

Garden Path

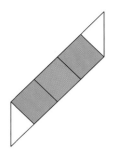

FIGURE 1. Unit A, make 130.

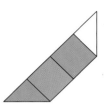

FIGURE 2. Unit B, make 10.

FIGURE 3. Unit C, make 10.

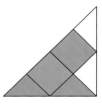

FIGURE 4. Unit D, make 10.

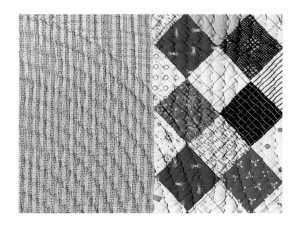

SEWING DIRECTIONS

PIECING THE PATCHWORK

✦ Sew three contrasting squares together. Sew two triangles to the ends of the pieced squares to make a diagonal row as shown (Unit A). Make 130 units. Press (Fig. 1).

✦ Sew two contrasting squares together. Sew two triangles to the ends of the pieced squares to make a diagonal row as shown (Unit B). Make 10 units. Press (Fig. 2).

✦ Sew two triangles together for row corners as shown (Unit C). Make 10 units. Press (Fig. 3).

PIECING THE PANELS

✦ Sew 26 of Unit A together diagonally, matching seams in each row. Make five rows. Press.

✦ Sew Unit C and Unit B as shown to make Unit D. Press. Make 10 of Unit D (Fig. 4).

✦ Sew Unit D to each end of the five pieced rows. Press (Fig. 5).

ASSEMBLING THE QUILT TOP

✦ Mark the pieced panels and sashing strips ¼" from the edge at each corner and at the half and quarter points.

✦ Arrange the panels and sashing strips, beginning and ending with a pink sashing strip. Pin and sew the pieced panels and sashing strips, matching marked points. Press.

FINISHING THE QUILT

✦ Mark the quilting design. The design used is an allover pattern called Shells or Baptist Fan. The curved lines are ¾" apart.

✦ Layer quilt top, batting, and backing, and baste.

✦ Quilt and bind.

✦ Sign and date your quilt.

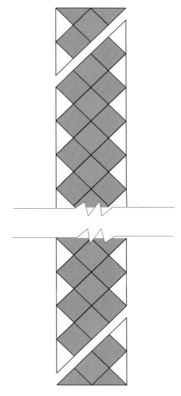

FIGURE 5. Sew 26 of Unit A together diagonally, make five rows. Sew Unit D to each end of all five rows.

QUILTING DESIGN

Shadow Boxes

SHADOW BOXES (50" x 56½"), BLOCK QUILTER UN-KNOWN, C. 1890, QUILT MADE BY BOBBIE AUG. Bobbie used vintage quilt blocks combined with reproduction fabrics to create this quilt.

QUILT SIZE 49½" x 54½" (93" x 97")

Note: Specifications in parenthesis are for the larger quilt size.

FABRIC REQUIREMENTS

SASHING AND BORDERS:
    1¾ yards (5½ yards) brown print

TRIANGLES D, SASHING, AND BORDERS:
    1¾ yards (3⅓ yards) blue print

TRIANGLES D:
    ⅔ yard (2 yards) alternate blue print

BACKING AND STRAIGHT-GRAIN BINDING:
    3¾ yards (9 yards) blue print
    Note: Backing is seamed horizontally.

PATCHWORK BLOCKS:
    Assorted prints and/or plaids
    Squares (A): ¼ yard (¾ yard)
    Squares (B): ⅜ yard (1 yard)
    Squares (C): ½ yard (1½ yards)

CUTTING LIST

BROWN PRINT:
    4 (4) strips 2½" x 38" (2½" x 81½") for top and bottom borders
    4 (10) strips 2½" x 43" (2½" x 85½") for sashing strips
    4 (4) strips 2½" x 55" (2½" x 97½") for side borders

(Cutting list continues on page 42)

Shadow Boxes

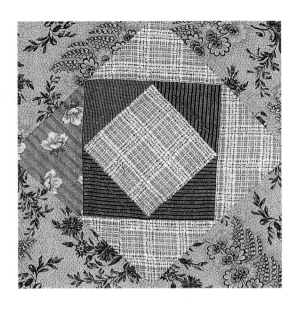

BLUE PRINT FOR BACKGROUND TRIANGLES, SASHING, AND BORDERS:

    2 (2) strips 2½" x 38" (2½" x 81½") for top and bottom borders

    2 (5) strips 2½" x 43" (2½" x 85½") for sashing strips

    2 (2) strips 2½" x 55" (2½" x 97½") for side borders

   7 (28) squares (D) 5⅛" x 5⅛", cut once diagonally

ALTERNATE BLUE PRINT FOR BACKGROUND TRIANGLES:

   23 (92) squares (D) 5⅛" x 5⅛", cut once diagonally

ASSORTED PRINTS FOR PATCHWORK BLOCKS:

    15 60) squares (A) 3½" x 3½"

   15 (60) squares (B) 4¼" x 4¼", cut twice diagonally

    30 (120) squares (C) 3⅞" x 3⅞", cut once diagonally

FIGURE 1. Sew triangles B to square A.

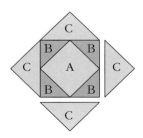

FIGURE 2. Sew triangles C to opposite sides of pieced square.

SEWING DIRECTIONS

PIECING THE BLOCKS

✦ Sew triangles (B) to opposite sides of square (A). Press seam allowances toward the square. Sew triangles (B) to remaining sides of square (A). Press allowances toward square (Fig. 1).

✦ Sew triangles (C) to opposite sides of pieced square. Press seam allowances toward square. Sew triangles (C) to remaining sides of square. Press allowances toward square (Fig. 2).

✦ Mix and match triangles (D) and sew to sides of pieced square as for C. Press seam allowances toward square. Make 15 (60) blocks (Fig. 3).

PIECING THE PANELS

✦ Make three (six) vertical rows of five (10) blocks each.

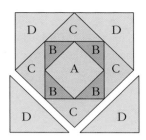

FIGURE 3. Sew triangles (D) to opposite sides of pieced square.

JOINING THE SASHING STRIPS

✦ Make two (five) triple-strip panels by joining one 2½" x 43" (2½" x 85½") brown strip to each side of a 2½" x 43" (2½" x 85½") blue strip.

ASSEMBLING THE QUILT TOP

✦ Mark sashing strips ¼" from the edge at each corner and at 8½" intervals.

✦ Arrange the three (six) panels and two (five) pieced sashing strips, beginning and ending with a panel. Pin and sew the pieced panels and sashing strips, matching the marked points with seams. Press.

ADDING THE TOP AND BOTTOM BORDERS

✦ Make two triple-strip panels by joining one 2½" x 38" (2½" x 81½") brown strip to each side of a 2½" x 38" (2½" x 81½") blue strip.

✦ Sew the top and bottom borders to the quilt as described in Adding Borders with Straight Corners, page 16.

ADDING THE SIDE BORDERS

✦ Make two triple-strip panels by joining one 2½" x 55" (2½" x 97½") brown strip to each side of a 2½" x 55" (2½" x 97½") blue strip.

✦ Sew the side borders to the quilt as described for straight corners on page 16.

FINISHING THE QUILT

✦ Mark the quilting design. The design used for this quilt is "by the piece," which means ¼" from the seam line inside each piece.

✦ Layer quilt top, batting, and backing, and baste.

✦ Quilt and bind.

✦ Sign and date your quilt.

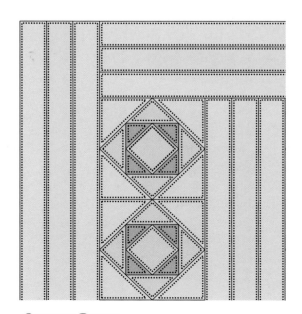

QUILTING DESIGN

Using Rectangles

Roman Coins

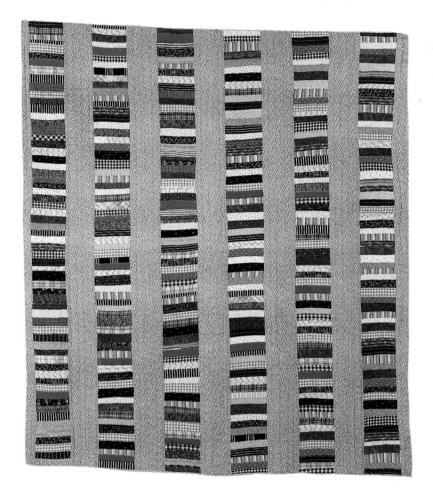

QUILT SIZE 77½" x 90"

FABRIC REQUIREMENTS

SASHING:
2¾ yards fabric

RECTANGLES:
3½ yards assorted prints

BACKING AND BINDING:
6 yards

CUTTING LIST

SASHING:
7 strips 6" x 90½"

ASSORTED PRINTS:
360 rectangles 2" x 7"

ROMAN COINS (70" x 84"), QUILTER UNKNOWN. A traditional quilt made in very early America. In addition to cotton, both silk and wool quilts have been made in this pattern. From the collection of Sharon Newman.

Roman Coins

SEWING DIRECTIONS

PIECING THE PANELS

✦ Mixing the colors and fabrics in each panel, sew 60 rectangles together along the long edges (refer to quilt photos). Make six panels.

ASSEMBLING THE QUILT TOP

✦ Mark sashing strips ¼" from the edge at each corner and at 1½" intervals.

✦ Arrange the panels and sashing strips, beginning and ending with a sashing strip. Pin and sew the pieced panels and sashing strips, matching marked points with the seams. Press.

FINISHING THE QUILT

✦ Mark the quilting design. This quilt has vertical lines in the sashing strips, ½" from the seams and 1½" apart. Diagonal lines are quilted over the patchwork.

✦ Layer quilt top, batting, and backing, and baste.

✦ Quilt and bind.

✦ Sign and date your quilt.

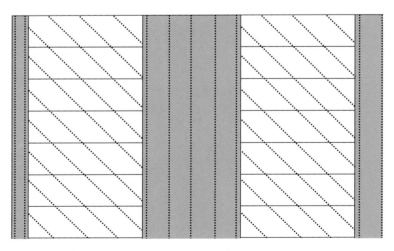

QUILTING DESIGN

Stacked Bricks

QUILT SIZE 73" x 78"

FABRIC REQUIREMENTS

SASHING:

2½ yards indigo print

BRICKS:

3¾ yards assorted prints

BACKGROUND:

1¾ yards

BACKING:

5 yards

BINDING:

¾ yard

CUTTING LIST

INDIGO PRINT:

6 strips 7" x 78½"

BACKGROUND:

440 squares 1⅞" x 1⅞"

ASSORTED PRINTS:

660 rectangles 1⅞" x 3¼" (folded in half crosswise and creased on each edge to mark the fold)

STACKED BRICKS (71" x 79½"), QUILTER UNKNOWN. In this quilt yellow prints used in each of the bars highlight a collection of fabrics from the fourth quarter of the nineteenth century. The dark indigo provides a good frame for the patchwork. From the collection of Sharon Newman.

SEWING DIRECTIONS

PIECING THE PANELS

✦ Sew three rectangles together along the short ends. Make 220 units (Fig. 1).

✦ Sew a square to each end of the rectangle units (Fig. 2).

✦ Using the crease mark in the centers of the rectangles to stagger the rows, assemble the pieced units into five vertical rows of 44 units (Fig. 3).

✦ Trim the long sides (Fig. 4) and top and bottom edges (Fig. 5) of the panels square, leaving a ¼" seam allowance, measured from the points.

ASSEMBLING THE QUILT TOP

✦ Mark the pieced panels and sashing strips ¼" from the edge at each corner and at the half, quarter, and eighth divisions.

✦ Arrange the panels and sashing strips, beginning and ending with a sashing strip. Pin and sew the pieced panels and sashing strips, matching marked points. Press.

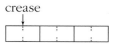

FIGURE 1. Sew three rectangles together, make 220 units.

FIGURE 2. Sew a square to each end of the units.

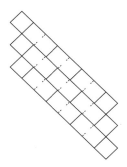

FIGURE 3. Assemble the pieced units into five vertical rows of 44 units.

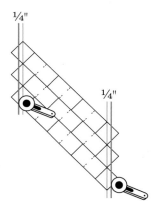

FIGURE 4. Trim long edges of panels, leaving a ¼" seam allowance.

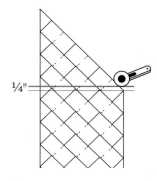

FIGURE 5. Trim top and bottom of panels, leaving a ¼" seam allowance.

Stacked Bricks

FINISHING THE QUILT

◆ Mark the quilting design. This allover design has diagonal lines quilted through the centers of the rectangles, extending over the sashing. Additional lines are quilted ¼" from the seams at the edge of the rectangles.

◆ Layer quilt top, batting, and backing, and baste.

◆ Quilt and bind.

◆ Sign and date your quilt.

QUILTING DESIGN

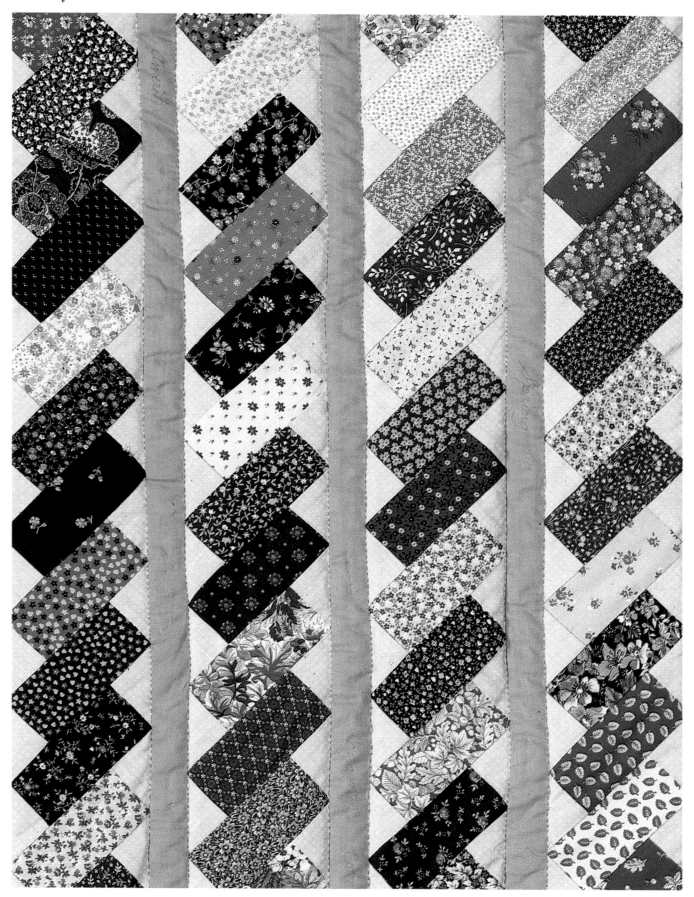

Stairway to Heaven

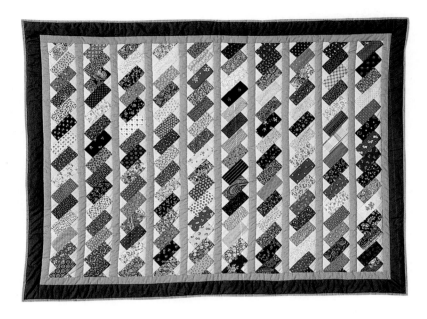

QUILT SIZE 47" x 37½"

FABRIC REQUIREMENTS

BORDER AND BINDING:

1½ yards

SASHING:

1⅜ yards

BACKGROUND:

1¼ yard

RECTANGLES:

1¼ yards assorted prints

BACKING:

1½ yards

CUTTING LIST

BORDER:

2 strips 2⅜" x 43⅜" for top and bottom

2 strips 2½" x 38"

SASHING:

11 strips 1½" x 32⅜"

2 strips 1½" x 43⅜"

BACKGROUND:

300 squares 2" x 2"

ASSORTED PRINTS:

150 rectangles 2" x 3½"

STAIRWAY TO HEAVEN (49" x 36"), MADE BY SHARON NEWMAN, 1998. The pieces sewn into this wall quilt are all samples received from fabric companies in the decade between 1979 and 1989. Early samples were cut about 2" x 4" and often were stapled together on one end. Names of many of the companies are written in the sashing.

SEWING DIRECTIONS

Fabric placement is the key to success with this pattern. Arrange column pieces without the background fabric and distribute the lights, darks, and similar prints to create a balanced layout.

PIECING THE PANELS

✦ Sew a square to each end of every rectangle. Make 150 pieced units (Fig. 1).

✦ Position one rectangle edge ¼" over the square on the adjacent rectangle. Sew 15 pieces units for each vertical row. Make 10 rows (Fig. 2).

✦ Slice column in two at some point. Match the last rectangle in one piece with the first in the other, and the column will be square at each end (Fig. 3).

✦ Trim the long edges of the panels, leaving a ¼" seam allowance, measured from the points (Fig. 4).

ASSEMBLING THE QUILT TOP

✦ Mark the pieced panels and sashing strips ¼" from the edge at each corner and at half, quarter, and eighth marks.

✦ Arrange the panels and sashing strips, beginning and ending with a sashing strip. Pin and sew the pieced panels and sashing strips, matching marked points. Press.

✦ Add the top and bottom strips of sashing fabric.

ADDING THE BORDERS

✦ Sew the outer border to the sides of quilt, then to the top and bottom, as described in Adding Borders with Straight Corners, page 16.

FIGURE 1. Sew a square to each end of rectangle, make 150 units.

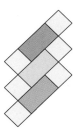

FIGURE 2. Sew 15 piece units for each row, make 10 rows.

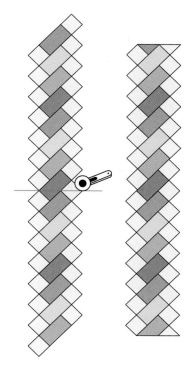

FIGURE 3. Make 5 vertical rows.

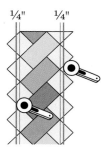

FIGURE 4. Trim edges leaving a ¼" seam allowance.

Stairway to Heaven

FINISHING THE QUILT

✦ Mark the quilting design. Stairway to Heaven is quilted in the ditch.

✦ Layer quilt top, batting, and backing, and baste.

✦ Quilt and bind.

✦ Sign and date your quilt.

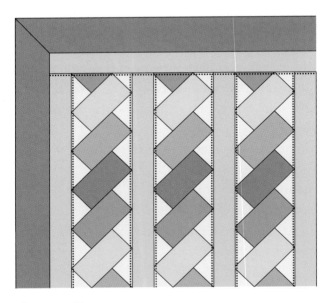

QUILTING DESIGN

SEVEN ROWS OF SCRAPS (66" X 82"), MADE BY SHARON NEWMAN, 1999. Sharon made this quilt from fabrics dating from 1978 to 1999. The bricks are 2½" x 6½", and the squares for the ends of the bricks are 2½" x 2½". Twenty-seven bricks are pieced together diagonally to form a row. Cutting across the patchwork, switching the two sections, and piecing the patchwork panel back together leave straight edges for the top and bottom of the row. The sashing strips are 3" and 4½" wide. There is a border at the top and bottom of the quilt. From the collection of Sharon Newman.

VERTICAL QUILTS WITH STYLE – BOBBIE AUG & SHARON NEWMAN

Using Triangles

Purple Sawtooth Bars

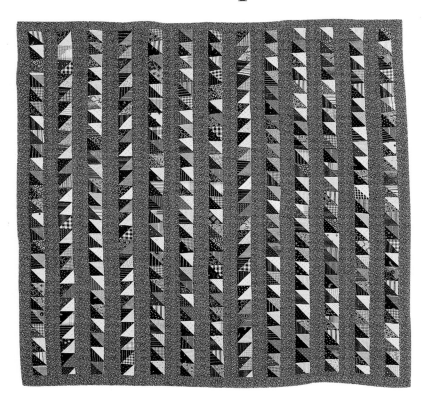

PURPLE SAWTOOTH BARS (78" x 81"), QUILTER UNKNOWN, C. 1890. This antique quilt is from Bobbie's collection. Oftentimes, large borders were added to increase the overall size of a quilt as well as showcase a particularly attractive floral print.

QUILT SIZE 81" x 81" (108" x 108")

Note: Specifications in parenthesis are for the larger quilt size. Feel free to add an additional outer border (cut 4½" wide) to the smaller quilt to make an 89" x 89" quilt.

FABRIC REQUIREMENTS

SASHING STRIPS AND BINDING:

5 yards (6¼ yards) purple

TRIANGLES:

2 yards (3 yards) assorted light prints

2 yards (3 yards) assorted dark prints

BACKING:

5 yards (10 yards)

CUTTING LIST

SASHING AND BINDING FABRIC:

14 strips 3½" x 75½" (4½" x 100½")

2 strips 3½" x 81½" (4½" x 108½") for top and bottom border

ASSORTED LIGHTS:

163 squares 3⅞" x 3⅞" (4⅞" x 4⅞")

ASSORTED DARKS:

163 squares 3⅞" x 3⅞" (4⅞" x 4⅞")

Purple Sawtooth Bars

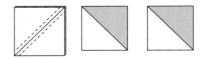

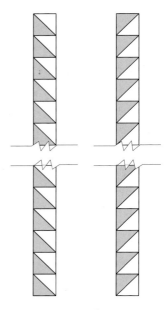

FIGURE 1. Half-square units, make 325 units.

FIGURE 2. Sew 25 pieced squares in a vertical row, make 13 rows.

SEWING DIRECTIONS

PIECING THE PANELS

✦ With right sides together, layer two 3⅞" (4⅞") squares, one light square and one dark square. Draw a diagonal line on the lighter square. Sew ¼" on each side of the line and then cut on the line to make the two half-square units. Make 325 units (Fig. 1).

✦ Sew 25 pieced squares into a vertical row as shown, with the dark half of the pieced square in the same position in the row. Make 13 rows. Press seam allowances to the dark triangles (Fig. 2).

ASSEMBLING THE QUILT TOP

✦ Mark sashing strips ¼" from the edge at each corner and at 3" (4") intervals.

✦ Arrange the panels and sashing strips, beginning and ending with a sashing strip. Pin and sew the pieced panels and sashing strips, matching the marked points with seams. Press.

ADDING THE TOP AND BOTTOM BORDERS

✦ Sew the top and bottom borders to the quilt as described in Adding Borders with Straight Corners, page 16.

FINISHING THE QUILT

✦ Mark the quilting design. The allover design for this quilt is diagonal lines, 1½" apart.

✦ Layer quilt top, batting, and backing, and baste.

✦ Quilt and bind.

✦ Sign and date your quilt.

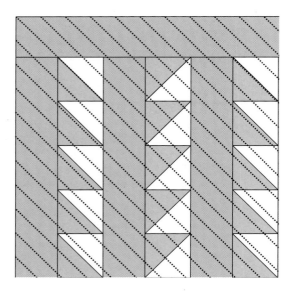

QUILTING DESIGN

Pleasure of Piecing

QUILT SIZE 73½" x 80"

FABRIC REQUIREMENTS

SASHING AND BINDING:

    5 yards

TRIANGLES:

    1¾ yards assorted light prints

    1¾ yards assorted dark prints

BACKING:

    5¼ yards

CUTTING LIST

SASHING:

    9 strips 6" x 69½"

    2 strips 6" x 74" for top and bottom borders

LIGHT PRINTS:

 94 squares 4¾" x 4¾", cut twice diagonally

DARK PRINTS:

 96 squares 4¾" x 4¾", cut twice diagonally

PLEASURE OF PIECING (79" x 89½"), MADE BY SHARON NEWMAN, 1998. The rickrack design of this quilt is created by the placement of light and dark triangles. Similar zigzag-patterned quilts can be found as early as 1830 with very large triangles of chintz prints.

SEWING DIRECTIONS

PIECING THE PANELS

✦ Beginning with a dark triangle, sew 47 triangles together in a vertical row as shown, alternating the light and dark triangles. Make eight rows (Fig. 1).

✦ Beginning with a light triangle, sew 47 triangles together in a vertical row as shown, alternating the light and dark triangles. Make eight rows (Fig. 2).

✦ Sew two rows of triangles together, a row beginning with a dark triangle and a row beginning with a light triangle. Match the points of the triangles in one row with the center of the long edge of the triangle in the second row. The ends will be ragged but will be trimmed later. Make eight pieced rickrack panels (Fig. 3).

ASSEMBLING THE QUILT TOP

✦ Trim each patchwork panel, allowing ¼" seam allowances beyond the whole dark triangle. There should be 23 whole dark triangles on one side and 23 light triangles on the other side of the panel (Fig. 4).

✦ Mark sashing strips ¼" from the edge at each corner and at 3" intervals.

✦ Arrange the panels and sashing strips, beginning and ending with a sashing strip. Pin and sew the pieced panels and sashing strips, matching the marked intervals and triangle points. Press.

ADDING THE BORDERS

✦ Add the top and bottom borders to the quilt as described in Adding Borders with Straight Corners, page 16.

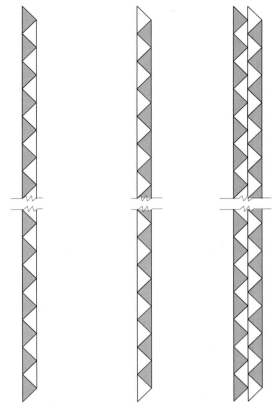

FIGURE 1.   **FIGURE 2.**   **FIGURE 3.**

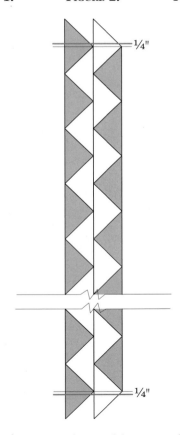

FIGURE 4. Trim each panel leaving a ¼" seam allowance.

The Pleasure of Piecing

My needle pricks the cloth,

Draws a line,

Joins and builds a patterned whole

From shapes I cut apart.

I love the work and cloth.

When I'm asked,

"Did you do this all by hand?"

I'll say, Oh no — by heart.

(Poem by Carol Cail)

✦ Mark the quilting design. The design used for this quilt is the words of a poem "The Pleasure of Piecing."

✦ Layer quilt top, batting, and backing, and baste.

✦ Quilt and bind.

✦ Sign and date your quilt.

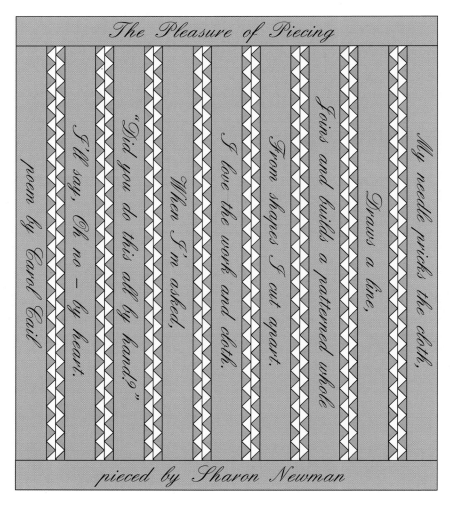

QUILTING DESIGN

1890S RICKRACK (75" x 82"), DETAIL, QUILTER UNKNOWN. Purchased from Shelly Zegart, this quilt top was probably made in Tennessee. Triangles measure about 2¼" on a side, and the bars are about 6" wide. Many browns from the late 1880s as well as shirtings and red from 1890 are included in the patchwork. From the collection of Sharon Newman.

1920S RICKRACK (76" x 92"), DETAIL, QUILTER UNKNOWN. Purchased from Mary Ann Walters in Texas, this quilt top contains a variety of prints. Note the difference that a light sashing gives the patchwork compared to dark sashings used in the other examples in this book. Triangles finish about 4¾" on a side, and the bars are 3¾" wide. From the collection of Sharon Newman.

Vertical Quilts with Style — Bobbie Aug & Sharon Newman

Tree Everlasting

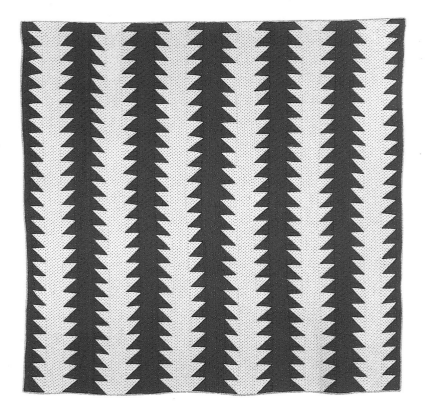

QUILT SIZE 70½" x 71½"

FABRIC REQUIREMENTS

BARS AND PATCHWORK:

2⅞ yards red with white dot

2⅞ yards white with black dot

BACKING AND BINDING:

5" yards pink print

CUTTING LIST

RED WITH WHITE DOT:

5 sashing strips 3½" x 72"

2 sashing strips 2" x 72"

156 squares 3⅝" x 3⅝"

WHITE WITH BLACK DOT:

6 sashing strips 3¾" x 72"

156 squares 3⅝" x 3⅝"

TREE EVERLASTING (70" x 70"), QUILTER UNKNOWN, C. 1900. This quilt is from Sharon's collection. The pattern, also known as Path of Thorns or Prickly Pear, has been well-documented in mid-nineteenth-century quilts. The design is characterized by its two-color alternating bars, divided by half-squares, which repeat the two colors in a way that appears like "branches."

Tree Everlasting

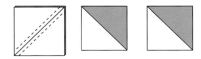

FIGURE 1. Half-square units, make 312.

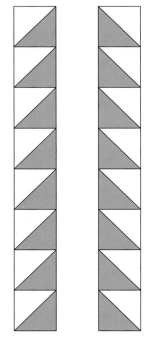

FIGURES 2 AND 3. Half-square units sewn in vertical rows.

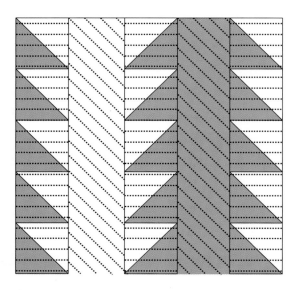

QUILTING DESIGN

SEWING DIRECTIONS

MAKING THE BRANCHES

✦ With right sides together, pair one light and one dark square. Draw a diagonal line on the light square. Sew ¼" from each side of the line and then cut on the line to make the two half-square units. Make 312 half-square units in all (Fig. 1).

✦ Arrange 26 half-squares so the dark triangle is in the lower right position. Sew into a vertical row. Make six rows in all (Fig. 2).

✦ Arrange 26 half-squares so the dark triangle is in the lower left position. Sew into a vertical row. Make six rows in all (Fig. 3).

PIECING THE PANELS

✦ Sew the rows of half-squares to the red sashing strips so the red side of the square touches the red sashing strip. Two rows of triangles sewn to each red sashing strip forms a "tree."

ASSEMBLING THE QUILT TOP

✦ Mark the white sashing strips ¼" from the edge at each corner and at 2¾" intervals.

✦ Arrange the remaining two rows of half-squares, the pieced panels, and the sashing strips as seen in the photo on page 65, beginning and ending with a row of half-squares.

✦ Pin and sew the red "tree" units to the white sashing strips, matching marked points with seams. Press.

✦ Sew the two rows of pieced squares to the outer white sashing strips, matching marked points with seams. Press.

FINISHING THE QUILT

✦ Mark the quilting design. The design for this quilt is ¾"
diagonal lines quilted over the bars with ¾" horizontal
lines quilted over the half-squares.

✦ Layer quilt top, batting, and backing, and baste.

✦ Quilt and bind.

✦ Sign and date your quilt.

PATH OF THORNS (79½" x 87"),
DETAIL, QUILTER UNKNOWN, C. 1900. This
quilt, with its pink printed chambray, was purchased from Mary Koval in 1997. The pink bars
are 7¼" wide, and the white polka dot bars are
8" wide. The half-squares are 3" finished. This
quilt is bordered on all sides with half-squares.
From the collection of Bobbie Aug.

RED AND WHITE PRICKLY PEAR
(83" x 76½"), DETAIL, QUILTER UN-
KNOWN, C. 1920. This quilt was purchased
from Mary Koval in 1997. Note the top and
bottom pieced borders. The white bars are
7½" wide, and the red bars are 7" wide. The
half-squares are 1½" finished. From the collection of Bobbie Aug.

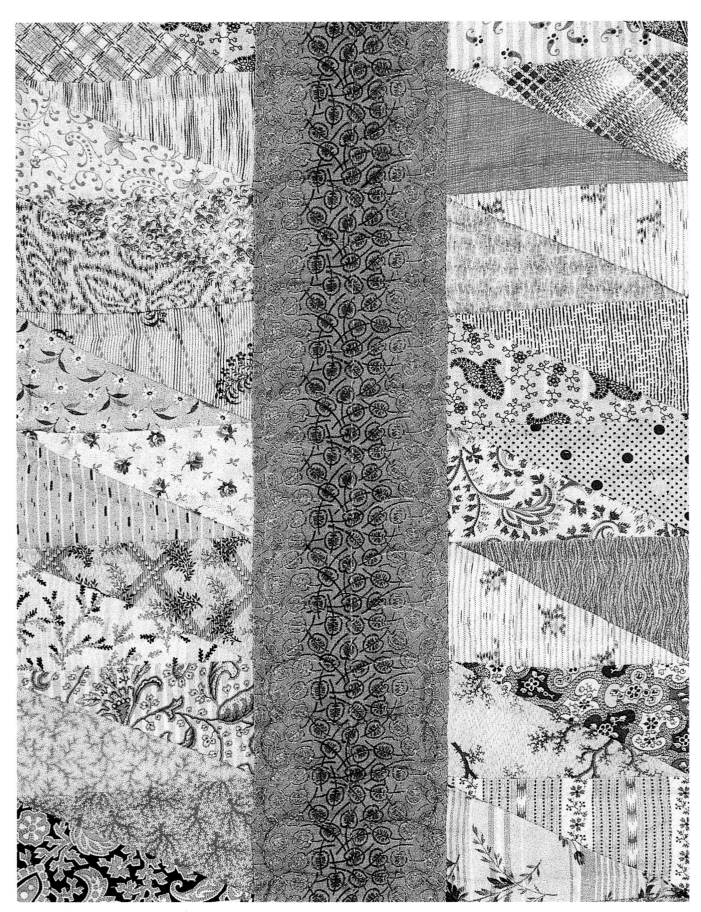

VERTICAL QUILTS WITH STYLE – BOBBIE AUG & SHARON NEWMAN

Triangle Treasures

TRIANGLE TREASURES (34½" x 39"), MADE BY BOBBIE AUG, 1998. Quilt top made from vintage triangles and new fabrics.

QUILT SIZE 33½" x 41¾" (87¾" x 104")

Note: Specifications in parenthesis are for the larger quilt size.

FABRIC REQUIREMENTS

BORDERS AND SASHING:

1⅛ yard (5 yards) blue

RECTANGLES AND ACCENT TRIANGLES:

1 yard (4¾ yards) assorted prints

BACKING AND BINDING:

1⅝ yards (9⅝ yards)

CUTTING LIST

SASHING AND BORDER FABRIC:

5 (7) strips 4" x 35¼" (6½" x 92⅝") for sashing and side borders

2 strips 4" x 27" (6½" x 76¼") for top and bottom borders

4 squares (A) 3" x 3" (4¾" x 4¾") for corner blocks

ACCENT FABRIC:

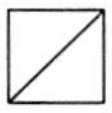

8 squares 2⅝" x 2⅝" (3⅞" x 3⅞") for corner blocks, cut once diagonally

ASSORTED PRINTS:

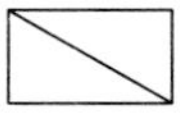

60 (132) rectangles 3" x 5⅛" (4⅞" x 8⅞"), all right side up, cut once diagonally

Triangle Treasures

FIGURE 1. Make 60 (132) pieced rectangles.

FIGURE 2. Sew 15 (22) pieced rectangles into vertical rows, make four (six) rows.

FIGURE 3. Sew accent triangles to opposite sides of square, make four blocks.

FIGURE 4. Sew a block to each end of top and bottom borders.

SEWING DIRECTIONS

PIECING THE PANELS

✦ With right sides together, sew two triangles along the long diagonal edge to form a rectangle. Be careful not to stretch the bias edges. Make 60 (132) pieced rectangles in all. Press seam allowances to the darkest fabric (Fig 1).

✦ Sew the long sides of 15 (22) pieced rectangles into a vertical row as shown. Make four (six) rows in all (Fig. 2).

ASSEMBLING THE QUILT TOP

✦ Mark the pieced panels and sashing strips ¼" from the edge at each corner and at half, quarter, and eighth marks.

✦ Arrange the panels and sashing strips, beginning and ending with a sashing strip. Pin and sew the pieced panels and sashing strips, matching marked points. Press.

ADDING THE TOP AND BOTTOM BORDERS

✦ Sew accent triangles to the opposite sides of a blue square. Press seam allowances toward the square. Sew accent triangles to the remaining sides of the square. Press seam allowances toward the square. Completed square should measure 4" (6½") including seam allowances. Make four blocks (Fig. 3).

✦ Sew a block to each end of the top and bottom borders (Fig. 4).

✦ Sew the top and bottom borders to the quilt as described in Adding Borders with Straight Corners, page 16.

FINISHING THE QUILT

✦ Mark the quilting design. The design used for this quilt is feathered vines in the sashing strips and outer borders, as well as lines ¼" from each side of the diagonal seam, alternating with lines ¼" inside of the rectangle shape. Corner blocks are quilted ¼" inside each shape.

✦ Layer quilt top, batting, and backing, and baste.

✦ Quilt and bind.

✦ Sign and date your quilt.

QUILTING DESIGN

VERTICAL QUILTS WITH STYLE – BOBBIE AUG & SHARON NEWMAN

Flying Geese

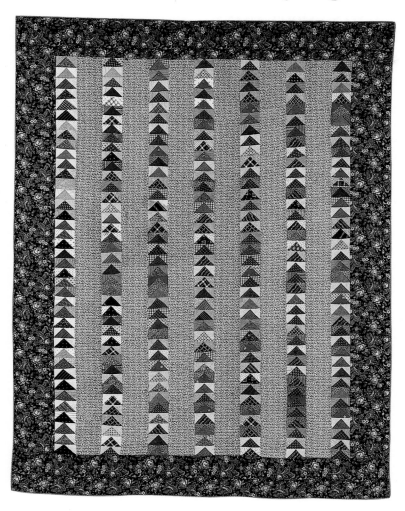

VERTICAL QUILTS WITH STYLE – BOBBIE AUG & SHARON NEWMAN

FLYING GEESE (84" x 110¼"), QUILT FINISHED BY BOBBIE AUG AND CAROLINE PETERSON, ATWOOD, KANSAS, QUILTED BY DOROTHY VICE, BEAVER CITY, NEBRASKA, 1998. Like so many vintage bar-set quilts, this top was without borders when Bobbie purchased it some years ago. She chose a large, brown floral, reminiscent of a nineteenth-century chintz, for the vintage over-sized borders. When Bobbie added the borders, she sewed straight corners rather than mitering them, in keeping with the style of this early quilt.

QUILT SIZE 87" x 107½"

FABRIC REQUIREMENTS

GEESE:
  3 yards assorted prints

SASHING BARS:
  2¾ yards brown print

BACKGROUND TRIANGLES:
  3¼ yards assorted prints

BORDERS:
  2⅞ yards large floral print

BACKING AND BINDING:
  10 yards

CUTTING LIST

SASHING FABRIC:
  6 strips 6¼" x 90½"

BORDER FABRIC:
  2 strips 9¼" x 90½" for side borders
  2 strips 9¼" x 87½" for top and bottom borders

FLYING GEESE (CORNER-SQUARE METHOD):
  32 strips 3" x 44", cut into 5½" segments. Cut 252 rectangles 3" x 5½".

BACKGROUND TRIANGLES:
  36 strips 3" x 44", cut into 3" units. Cut 504 squares 3" x 3".

Flying Geese

FIGURE 1. Sew on the fold line and cut off the triangles.

FIGURE 2. Press triangle open.

FIGURE 3. Repeat for the other side.

FIGURE 4. Completed unit.

SEWING DIRECTIONS

PIECING THE GEESE

✦ With wrong sides together, lightly press a square in half diagonally.

✦ Open the square and lay it with right sides together on top of one end of a rectangle, aligning two sides as shown. Stitch diagonally on the fold line. Trim seam allowance to ¼" (Fig. 1).

✦ Fold the triangle over the stitching line. Press (Fig. 2).

✦ Repeat Steps 1 through 3 using another square on the opposite end of the rectangle as shown (Fig. 3).

✦ This forms the pieced geese unit. Make 252 pieced geese units (Fig. 4).

PIECING THE PANELS

✦ Arrange the pieced geese units, with all the geese going the same direction. Sew 36 units together to form a row. Make seven rows in all.

ASSEMBLING THE QUILT TOP

✦ Mark the pieced panels and sashing strips ¼" from the edge at each corner and at 2½" intervals.

✦ Arrange the pieced panels and sashing strips, beginning and ending with a pieced panel. Pin and sew the pieced panels and sashing strips, matching marked points. Press.

ADDING THE BORDERS

✦ Sew the side borders to the quilt top as described in Adding Borders with Straight Corners, page 16. Press.

✦ Sew the top and bottom borders to the quilt.

FINISHING THE QUILT

✦ Mark the quilting design. The sashing strips and borders were quilted with a cable and feather design. The geese were quilted ¼" by the piece. The pieced panels were quilted in the ditch.

✦ Layer quilt top, batting, and backing, and baste.

✦ Quilt and bind.

✦ Sign and date your quilt.

QUILTING DESIGN

Flying Geese

A.K.A. WILD GOOSE CHASE, WILD GEESE FLYING, GEESE IN FLIGHT

One of the earliest bar quilt patterns from the nineteenth century is called Flying Geese. Each rectangular unit consists of a large triangle (the "goose") and two smaller triangles, one on either side of the goose, as the background. The size of the basic unit and the width of the setting bars can vary greatly.

If the geese and the background fabrics are the same value, the geese will be unobtrusive. If the geese and the background are of different or contrasting values, the geese will attract attention and your eye will follow their flight pattern. Feel free to use many different fabrics for the geese and the background triangles. A scrappy look can be very effective. The background can be light or dark or change from row to row. The geese can all go one direction or the rows can alternate.

The sashing strips provide another opportunity for contrast in color and value. In early quilts, large florals and bold stripes were popular. Today, you can choose almost anything for the sashing strips. Yardage required will depend on the size of the quilt, the number and width of sashing strips, as well as the number of repeats in the print, if you choose a stripe or something similar.

No matter what fabrics you choose, your quilt is bound to be wonderful when it's a Flying Geese!

GOLDEN GEESE (68" x 82"), DETAIL, QUILTER UNKNOWN. The golden yellow fabric for the geese has holes, indicating it was a sacking fabric. The 5½"-wide blue sashing is an unwashed glazed print. The geese are 2¼" x 4½". This quilt is a good example of the type made in the first quarter of the twentieth century. From the collection of Sharon Newman.

TRIPLE-SASHED FLYING GEESE (74" X 87"), DETAIL, QUILTER UNKNOWN. This quilt dates from the fourth quarter of the nineteenth century. The 2½" x 5" geese are light prints with dark print backgrounds. The red gingham and white with black polka dot sashing strips are 2½" finished. From the collection of Sharon Newman.

FOLK ART GEESE (80½" x 89"), DETAIL, QUILTER UNKNOWN. Although there are many mid-nineteenth-century fabrics in this top, it was probably completed around 1870. The 6"-wide border print stripe works well in the bars. The pieced panels measure 6½" wide. From the collection of Bobbie Aug.

Vertical Quilts with Style – Bobbie Aug & Sharon Newman

Delectable Mountains

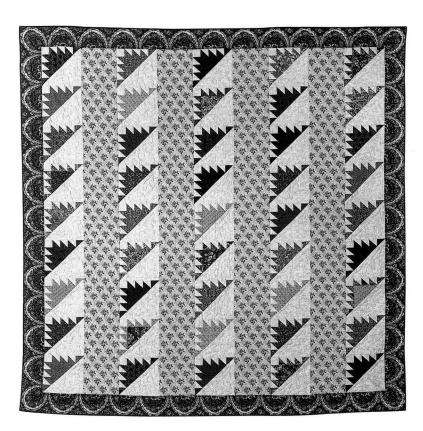

QUILT SIZE 98" x 102"

FABRIC REQUIREMENTS

BACKGROUND:

3¾ yards cream print

SASHING:

2¾ yards pink floral print

BORDER:

3 yards blue print

PATCHWORK:

3 yards assorted prints

BACKING:

9 yards

BINDING:

1 yard

CUTTING LIST

BACKGROUND:

 23 squares 10⅞" x 10⅞", cut once diagonally for 46 triangles (one will be extra)

135 squares 2⅞" x 2⅞"

45 squares 2½" x 2½"

SASHING:

4 strips 9½" x 90½"

BORDERS:

2 strips 6½" x 98½" for top and bottom

2 strips 6½" x 102½" for sides

ASSORTED PRINTS:

 23 squares 6⅞" x 6⅞", cut once diagonally to make 46 triangles (one will be extra)

135 squares 2⅞" x 2⅞" (6 squares of the same print for each of the 45 triangles above)

 45 squares 2⅞" x 2⅞", cut once diagonally

1 square of the same print for each of the 23 larger print squares

DELECTABLE MOUNTAINS (98" x 102"), MADE BY SHARON NEWMAN, 1998. This quilt was inspired by a quilt made in New York State in 1845. This pieced block is found in many early quilts in several different arrangements.

Delectable Mountains

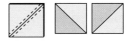

FIGURE 1. Make 45 sets of six half-square units each.

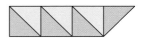

FIGURE 2. Unit A, make 45.

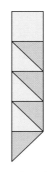

FIGURE 3. Unit B, make 45.

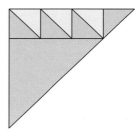

FIGURE 4. Sew Unit A to short side of large print triangle.

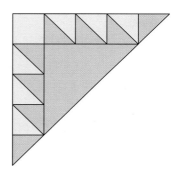

FIGURE 5. Sew Unit B to short side of large print triangle to complete Unit C.

SEWING DIRECTIONS

MAKING THE HALF-SQUARE UNITS

✦ With right sides together, layer two 2⅞" squares (one from the background fabric and one from the assorted prints). Draw a diagonal line on the lighter square. Sew ¼" on each side of the line and then cut on the line to make the two half-square units. Make 45 sets of six half-square units each (Fig. 1).

PIECING THE BLOCKS

✦ Sew three half-square units and one print triangle together as shown. Make 45 of Unit A (Fig. 2).

✦ Sew three half-square units, one print triangle, and one background square as shown. Make 45 of Unit B (Fig. 3).

✦ Sew Unit A to short side of large print triangle. Press (Fig. 4).

✦ Sew Unit B to other short side of large print triangle to complete Unit C. Press (Fig. 5).

✦ With right sides together, sew the large background triangle to Unit C, matching edges. Stitch the long sides together. Press the seam allowance away from background. Make 45 blocks (Fig. 6).

PIECING THE PANELS

✦ Arrange nine blocks in a vertical row, with the dark side of each block in the upper-left corner. Sew together and press. Make five rows.

ASSEMBLING THE QUILT TOP

✦ Mark sashing strips ¼" from the edge at each corner and at 10" intervals.

◆ Arrange the panels and sashing strips, beginning and ending with a pieced panel. Pin and sew the pieced panels and sashing strips, matching marked points with seams. Press.

ADDING THE BORDERS

◆ Add the side, top, and bottom borders to the quilt as described in Adding Borders with Mitered Corners, page 16.

FINISHING THE QUILT

◆ Mark the quilting design. For this quilt there are four lines of cable in the sashing strips. The patchwork is quilted in the ditch with a decorative motif in the cream background. The border is quilted in the outline of the print.

◆ Layer quilt top, batting, and backing, and baste.

◆ Quilt and bind.

◆ Sign and date your quilt.

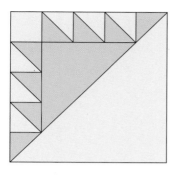

FIGURE 6. Sew large background triangle to Unit C, make 45 blocks.

QUILTING DESIGN

DELECTABLE MOUNTAINS Full-size Quilting Pattern

Vertical Quilts with Style – Bobbie Aug & Sharon Newman

Other Patterns

VERTICAL QUILTS WITH STYLE — BOBBIE AUG & SHARON NEWMAN

Bicentennial Baskets

BICENTENNIAL BASKETS (62" x 72"), MADE BY CARLA TOCZEK, 1998. Inspired by an antique basket quilt, Carla drafted the block and designed this vertical setting. The fabrics are a mix of reproduction prints. The appliqué of the handles is the only handwork in the blocks. One hand-quilted block sits amidst the machine quilting.

QUILT SIZE 62½" x 73¾"

FABRIC REQUIREMENTS

BASKETS:

    5 fat eighths of red prints
    5 fat eighths of blue

BASKETS AND BORDER:

    2¼ yards plaid

BACKGROUND:

    2 yards ivory

BARS:

    2 yards floral print

SASHING BARS AND BINDING:

    2 yards dark blue print

BORDER:

    ⅓ yard red print

BACKING:

    4 yards

CUTTING LIST

RED PRINTS:

    10 squares 2" x 2"
    15 squares 2⅜" x 2⅜", cut once diagonally
    5 bias strips ¾" x 12" for basket handles

RED PRINT FOR BORDER:

    8 strips 1" x 44"

BLUE PRINTS:

    10 squares 2" x 2"
    15 squares 2⅜" x 2⅜", cut once diagonally
    5   bias strips ¾" x 12" for basket handles

(Cutting list continues on page 86)

Bicentennial Baskets

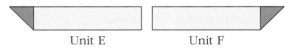

Unit E   Unit F

FIGURE 1. Make 5 unit E's and 5 unit F's with red, make 5 unit E's and 5 unit F's with blue.

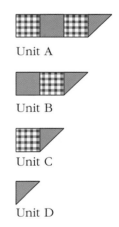

Unit A

Unit B

Unit C

Unit D

FIGURE 2. Make 5 red and 5 blue of these combinations.

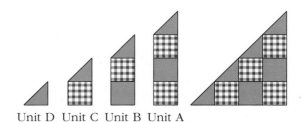

Unit D   Unit C   Unit B   Unit A

FIGURE 3. Piece units together to construct basket.

PLAID:
2   strips 3½" x 76" for sides
2   strips 3½" x 65" for top and bottom
40 squares 2" x 2"

IVORY BACKGROUND FABRIC:
5   squares 3⅞" x 3⅞" for base, cut once diagonally
20 rectangles 2" x 7"
5   squares 9⅞" x 9⅞" for top of baskets, cut once diagonally
4   squares 14" x 14" for setting triangles, cut twice diagonally
4   squares 7¼" x 7¼" for corners, cut once diagonally

FLORAL PRINT:
3   sashing strips 7½" x 64¼"

DARK BLUE PRINT:
6   strips 2" x 64¼" for vertical sashing
2   strips 2" x 56" for top and bottom sashing

SEWING DIRECTIONS
Note: There are many bias edges in this quilt. Use care in sewing and pressing.

PIECING THE BASKETS
✦ Sew two print triangles to two ivory rectangles, as shown. Make 5 unit E's and 5 unit F's with red, make 5 unit E's and 5 unit F's with blue (Fig. 1).

◆ Make five red and five blue of the following combinations (Fig. 2):

    A. plaid square, print square, plaid square, print triangle

    B. print square, plaid square, print triangle

    C. plaid square, print triangle

    D. print triangle

◆ Piece units together to construct basket (Fig. 3).

◆ Sew E and F to sides of basket (Fig. 4).

◆ Use a straight edge to trim rectangles even with the top of basket (Fig. 5).

◆ Sew small ivory triangle to base of basket (Fig. 6).

◆ For the handles, fold a crease to mark the center of each bias strip. Shape the bias strips on the large ivory triangles with the crease at center of the triangle (Fig. 7).

◆ Turn under the edges and appliqué with a blind stitch. Trim excess bias at edge of triangle.

◆ Sew top of basket to bottom triangle using care not to stretch bias edges. Press carefully. Make ten baskets (Fig. 8, page 88).

Piecing the Panels

◆ Arrange basket blocks into rows according to color. Add corner triangles to the top and bottom half of each top block. Press.

◆ Add side and corner triangles as shown in Fig. 9, on page 88.

◆ Sew the five baskets together for each of two vertical rows.

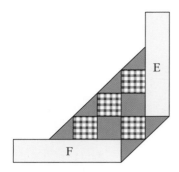

FIGURE 4. Sew Units E and F to sides of basket.

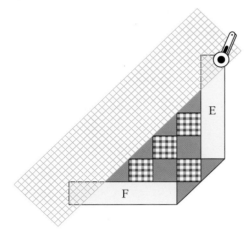

FIGURE 5. Trim rectangles even with top of basket.

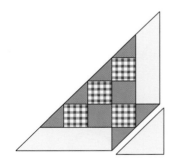

FIGURE 6. Sew triangle to base of basket.

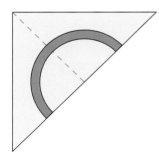

FIGURE 7. Shape bias strip on large triangle for handle.

Bicentennial Baskets

FIGURE 8. Sew top and bottom of basket together, make 10 baskets.

FIGURE 9. Add triangles and sew in diagonal rows.

ASSEMBLING THE QUILT TOP

✦ Sew a dark blue strip to each side of the floral sashing strips. Press.

✦ Mark sashing strips at ¼" and 6⅜" at each end. Mark 12¾" intervals in between.

✦ Arrange sashing strips and pieced panels, beginning and ending with a sashing strip. Pin and sew the sashing strips and pieced panels, matching marked points with seams. Press.

✦ Sew dark blue strips to the top and bottom of quilt as described in Adding Borders with Straight Corners, page 16. Press.

ADDING THE BORDERS

Note: For each border, center and sew the strip to the quilt, leaving the ends unfinished. You will miter all the borders at once.

✦ Piece the red print strips, end to end, and cut two strips 1" x 60" and two strips 1" x 70" from the pieced strip.

✦ Add red print and plaid borders to quilt as described in Adding Borders with Mitered Corners, page 16. Press.

FINISHING THE QUILT

✦ Mark the quilting design. This quilt has an interlocking design of squares quilted into the bars and setting triangles. The baskets have been outlined ¼" outside the seam line. Lines cross the plaid squares and sunrays fill the interior of the handle from the center of the top of the basket.

✦ Layer quilt top, batting, and backing, and baste.

✦ Quilt and bind.

✦ Sign and date your quilt.

QUILTING DESIGN

VERTICAL QUILTS WITH STYLE – BOBBIE AUG & SHARON NEWMAN

Hill and Valley

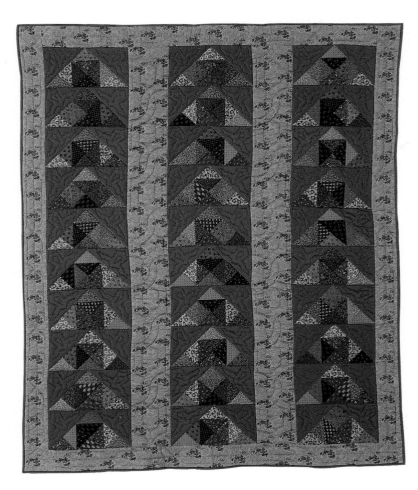

HILL AND VALLEY (48" x 59"), MADE BY SHARON NEWMAN AND QUILTED BY D. GARRISON, 1998. This pattern was copyrighted in 1933 and appeared in the Nancy Page Quilt Scrapbook Club of printed quilt patterns through Publishers Syndicate. The pieced units can be found arranged as they are in this pattern, or in horizontal or vertical rows alternated with a similar background triangle.

QUILT SIZE 47½" x 58½"

FABRIC REQUIREMENTS

SASHING:

1¾ yards print

BACKGROUND AND BINDING:

1½ yards

TRIANGLES:

45 assorted prints

BACKING:

3 yards

CUTTING LIST

SASHING AND BORDER PRINT:

2 sashing strips 5½" x 53"

2 strips 3½" x 42" for top and bottom borders

2 strips 3½" x 59" for side borders

BACKGROUND:

 30 squares 6⅛" x 6⅛", cut once diagonally for 60 triangles

ASSORTED PRINTS:

45 squares 3⅜" x 3⅜" cut once diagonally for 90 triangles

90 squares 3⅜" x 3⅜"

Hill and Valley

FIGURE 1. Half-square units, make 90 units.

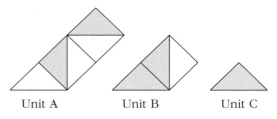

Unit A   Unit B   Unit C

FIGURE 2. Assemble 30 of Unit A, 30 of Unit B, and 30 of Unit C.

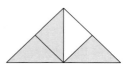

FIGURE 3. Sew Unit C to Unit B, make 30 pieced triangles.

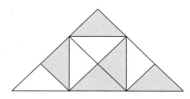

FIGURE 4. Sew Units B and C to Unit A, make 30 pieced triangles.

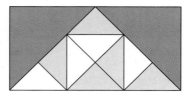

FIGURE 5. Sew background triangles to each of the 30 pieced triangles.

SEWING DIRECTIONS

PIECING THE BLOCKS

✦ With right sides together, layer two 3⅜" squares. Draw a diagonal line on the lighter square. Sew ¼" on each side of the line and then cut on the line to make the two half-square units. Make 90 half-squares (Fig. 1).

✦ Pick colors that blend and work variety into the sets. Assemble 30 of Unit A, 30 of Unit B, and 30 of Unit C. Sew the units together as illustrated (Fig. 2).

✦ Sew Unit C to Unit B as shown. Press. Make 30 pieced triangles (Fig. 3).

✦ Sew Unit B+C to Unit A as illustrated. Press. Make 30 pieced triangles (Fig. 4).

✦ Sew background triangles to each of the pieced triangles. Press. You should have 30 pieced rectangles (Fig. 5).

PIECING THE PANELS

✦ Sew 10 pieced rectangles into vertical rows. Make three rows.

ASSEMBLING THE QUILT TOP

✦ Mark sashing strips ¼" from the edge at the corners and at 5¼" intervals.

✦ Arrange the sashing strips and pieced panels, beginning and ending with a pieced panel. Pin and sew the sashing strips and panels, matching marked points with seams. Press.

ADDING THE BORDERS

✦ Mark the intervals on the top and bottom borders as follows: ¼", 10½", 5", 10½", 5", 10½", ¼". Pin and sew the top and bottom borders to the quilt, matching marked points with seams. Press.

✦ Mark side borders ¼" and 3" from both ends. Mark center secton in 5¼" intervals. Pin and sew the side borders to the quilt, matching marked points with seams. Press.

FINISHING THE QUILT

✦ Mark the quilting design. This quilt has an "X" quilted through the patchwork with a decorative motif in the background of the rectangles. The bars are quilted in an interlocking, double-line, square cable, and the border is quilted in a twisted, single-line, square cable.

✦ Layer quilt top, batting, and backing, and baste.

✦ Quilt and bind.

✦ Sign and date your quilt.

QUILTING DESIGN

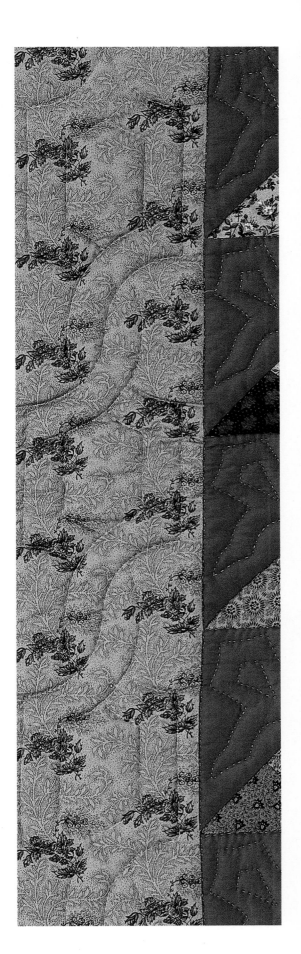

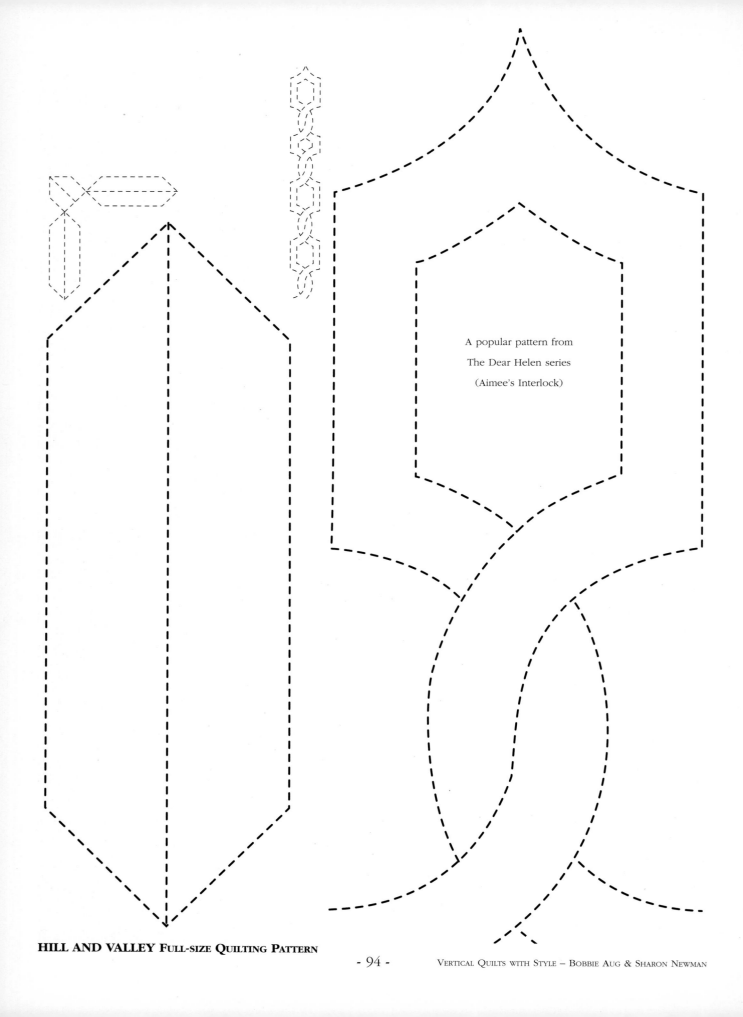

A popular pattern from
The Dear Helen series
(Aimee's Interlock)

HILL AND VALLEY **Full-size Quilting Pattern**

Vertical Quilts with Style — Bobbie Aug & Sharon Newman

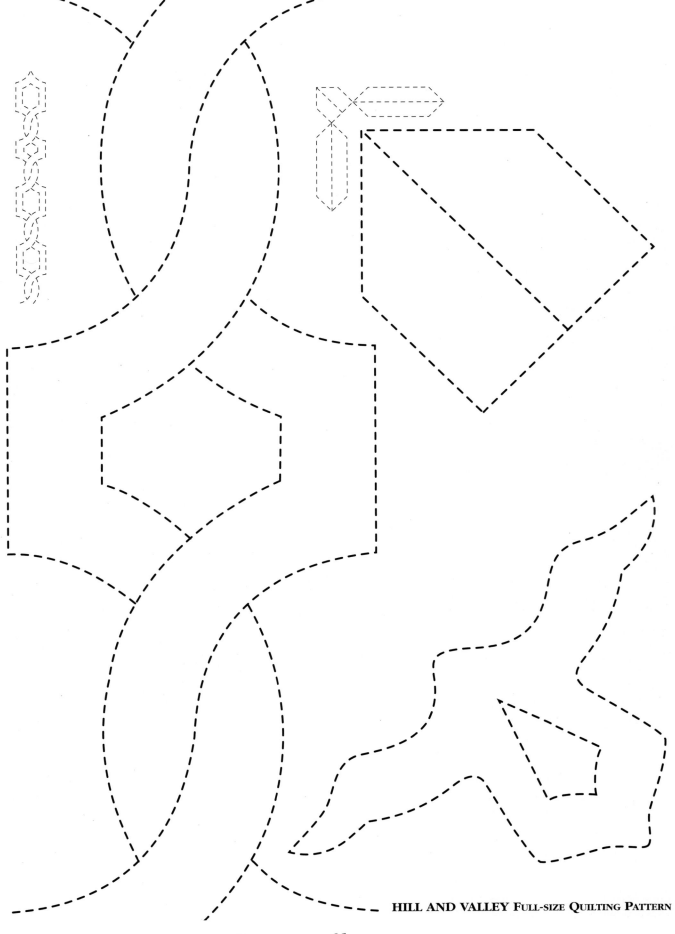

HILL AND VALLEY FULL-SIZE QUILTING PATTERN

Turn-of-the-Century Redwork

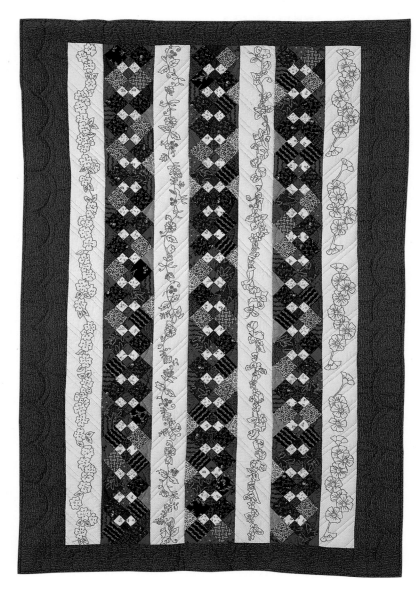

QUILT SIZE 44" x 65⅞"

FABRIC REQUIREMENTS
MUSLIN:
> 2 yards

BORDER AND BINDING:
> 2 yards red print

FOUR-PATCHES:
> ⅓ yard assorted light prints
> ⅔ yard assorted red prints
> ½ yard assorted indigo prints

EMBROIDERY:
> 12 skeins red embroidery floss

CUTTING LIST
MUSLIN:
> 1 piece 24" x 65"

BORDER PRINT:
> 2 strips 3¾" x 44½"
> 2 strips 6" x 59⅞"

LIGHT PRINTS:
> 5 strips 1½" x 42"

RED PRINTS:
> 5 strips 1½" x 42"
> 32 squares 4⅛" x 4⅛", cut diagonally twice
> 6 squares 2⅜" x 2⅜", cut diagonally once

INDIGO PRINTS:
> 126 squares 2½" x 2½"

TURN-OF-THE-CENTURY REDWORK (42" x 64"), MADE BY SHARON NEWMAN, QUILTED BY D. GARRISON, 1999. Redwork embroidery started as early as 1860, but it was very popular in the latter part of the nineteenth century. Designs included flowers, pets, and household items. Many times the blocks were marked and sold for one cent and were therefore called "penny squares." Linens, such as pillowcases, shams, and dresser scarves, were also embroidered. This quilt was inspired by redwork quilts made 100 years ago.

Turn-of-the-Century Redwork

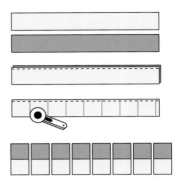

FIGURE 1. Cut 1½" segments.

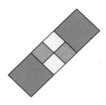

FIGURE 2. Make 60 four-patch units.

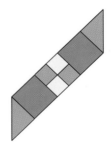

FIGURE 3. Sew indigo squares to the four-patch units.

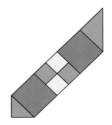

FIGURE 4. Add red triangles.

FIGURE 5. Make six units like these.

SEWING DIRECTIONS

PIECING THE FOUR-PATCHES

✦ With right sides together, sew a red strip and a light strip together lengthwise. Make five paired strips. Press seam allowances toward the red.

✦ Cut the pieced strips into 1½" segments. Cut 120 segments (Fig. 1).

✦ Sew two segments together as shown to make a four-patch unit. Make 60 four-patches (Fig. 2).

PIECING THE PANELS

✦ Sew indigo squares on opposite sides of a four-patch unit. Make 60 of these units (Fig. 3).

✦ Sew red triangles to 54 of the pieced units as shown in Figure 4.

✦ Make six units that have a side triangle and a corner triangle (Fig. 5).

✦ To the remaining six indigo squares, sew red triangles on three sides (Fig. 6).

✦ Arrange the pieced units as shown in Figure 7. Piece three vertical rows with 20 Four-Patches each. Add corner units to top left and bottom right of the rows.

EMBROIDERING THE SASHING STRIPS

✦ On the piece of muslin, mark four strips 4½" x 59½" for the redwork. Trace the redwork designs on the muslin strips.

✦ Embroider redwork using two strands of floss and the basic outline stitch.

✦ Cut redwork strips apart.

ASSEMBLING THE QUILT TOP

✦ Mark the pieced panels and sashing strips ¼" from the edge at each corner and at equal intervals.

✦ Arrange the pieced panels and embroidered sashing strips, beginning and ending with a sashing strip. Pin and sew the strips and panels together, matching marked points. Press.

ADDING THE BORDERS

✦ Sew the top and bottom borders to the quilt as described in Adding Borders with Straight Corners, page 16. Press.

✦ Sew the side borders to the quilt. Press.

FINISHING THE QUILT

✦ Mark the quilting design. This quilt has a pair of double lines quilted over the redwork. A cable design is quilted over the patchwork panels.

✦ Layer quilt top, batting, and backing, and baste.

✦ Quilt and bind.

✦ Sign and date your quilt.

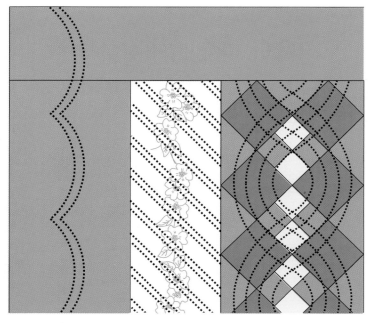

QUILTING DESIGN

FIGURE 6. Sew red triangles to remaining six squares.

FIGURE 7. Piece three vertical rows with 20 Four patches each.

outline stitch

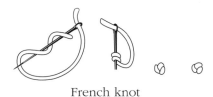

French knot

EMBROIDERY STITCHES

Outline stitch: Bring needle up at the end of line to be covered. Insert needle a short distance to the right and bring it out a little way to the left at a slight angle. Keep the thread above the needle.

French knot: Bring the needle up at a point where the knot is to be made. Wrap the thread two or three times around the point of needle. Insert it in the fabric as close as possible to the spot where the thread emerges (but not in the exact spot) and pull it to the wrong side, holding the wraps in place.

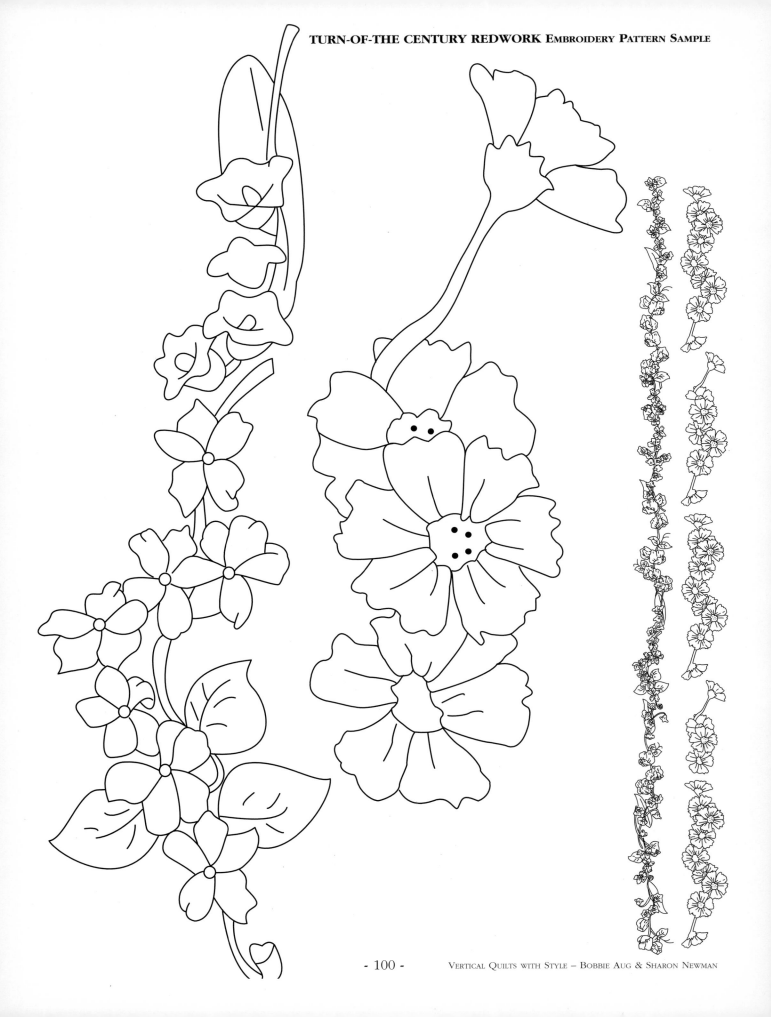

Vᴇʀᴛɪᴄᴀʟ Qᴜɪʟᴛs ᴡɪᴛʜ Sᴛʏʟᴇ – Bᴏʙʙɪᴇ Aᴜɢ & Sʜᴀʀᴏɴ Nᴇᴡᴍᴀɴ

VERTICAL QUILTS WITH STYLE – BOBBIE AUG & SHARON NEWMAN

Desert Garden

QUILT SIZE 92" x 92"

FABRIC REQUIREMENTS

BACKGROUND TRIANGLES:
3¾ yards floral print

TRIANGLES:
½ yard each of ten different colored prints

BORDER AND BINDING:
3 yards purple print

BORDER INSERT:
⅓ yard gold print

BACKING:
8½ yards fabric

CUTTING LIST

FLORAL FABRIC:
200 squares 4⅞" x 4⅞", cut once diagonally

TEN DIFFERENT COLORED PRINT FABRICS:
20 squares from each print 4⅞" x 4⅞", cut once diagonally

PURPLE BORDER FABRIC:
2 strips 6½" x 95" for top and bottom mitered borders

4 strips 6½" x 27½"

4 strips 1½" x 40½"

40 squares 2⅞" x 2⅞", cut once diagonally

GOLD BORDER FABRIC:
40 squares 2⅞" x 2⅞", cut once diagonally

DESERT GARDEN (92" x 92"), MADE BY GWEN OBERG, 1999. Our good friend Gwen Oberg was the maker of this gorgeous quilt. Gwen and her husband Steve reside in Albuquerque, New Mexico, and I think those beautiful New Mexican sunsets might have influenced Gwen just a little! She is a wonderful quiltmaker with an excellent eye for color arrangement and has a style all her own.

Desert Garden

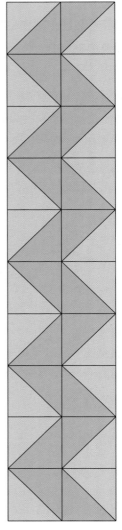

Arrange squares in a zigzag.

SEWING DIRECTIONS

PIECING THE PANELS

✦ Sew a floral triangle and a print triangle together to make a 4½" square, including seam allowances. Press seam allowances in the same direction. Make 40 squares for each of the 10 fabrics, 400 squares in all.

✦ Each zigzag is formed by making a panel two squares wide and 20 squares long. Arrange the squares in zigzag fashion as shown in the figure.

✦ Sew 20 squares together to form the first vertical row. Press.

✦ Sew 20 squares together to form the second vertical row. Press.

✦ Sew the first and second rows together to complete the panel. Press.

✦ Repeat for each of the nine remaining colors.

ASSEMBLING THE QUILT TOP

✦ Arrange the panels as desired. Pin and sew the panels together, matching seams. Press.

PIECING THE SIDE BORDERS

✦ Sew a purple triangle and a gold triangle together to make a 2½" square, including seam allowances. Make 80 squares in all. Press seam allowances in the same direction.

✦ Sew 20 squares together to form the first row. Press.

✦ Sew 20 squares together to form the second row. Press.

✦ Sew the first and second rows together to complete the border panel. Press.

✦ Repeat steps 2 through 4 for the second border panel. Press.

✦ Sew a 1½"-wide strip to each long side of the zigzag panels. Press.

✦ To complete the side borders, sew a 6½"-wide strip to each end of the zigzag panels. Press.

ADDING THE BORDERS
✦ Add the side, top, and bottom borders as described in Adding Borders with Mitered Corners, page 16.

FINISHING THE QUILT
✦ Mark the quilting design. DESERT GARDEN was quilted in a zigzag design, in the ditch along the zigzag seam lines, and continuing to the top and bottom borders. The two side borders were quilted in the same zigzag fashion, in the ditch of the zigzag inset, and continuing to the top and bottom of the quilt.

✦ Layer quilt top, batting, and backing, and baste.

✦ Quilt and bind.

✦ Sign and date your quilt.

QUILTING DESIGN

VERTICAL QUILTS WITH STYLE – BOBBIE AUG & SHARON NEWMAN

Log Cabin

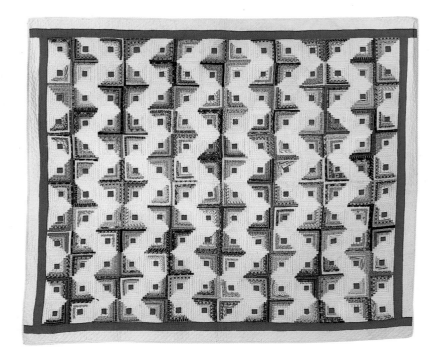

LOG CABIN (98" x 66¾"), QUILTER UNKNOWN. A favorite pattern for many decades, the Log Cabin is loved for the versatility of the settings that can be made with this simple-to-piece block. The maker of this quilt created vertical designs by a straight-set, repetitive pattern. From the collection of Sharon Newman.

QUILT SIZE 96½" x 96½"

FABRIC REQUIREMENTS

BLOCKS, BORDER AND BINDING:

8 yards white

BLOCKS:

6 yards assorted medium and dark prints

CENTERS AND BORDER:

3 yards red

BACKING:

9 yards white

CUTTING LIST

RED:

2 strips 2¼" x 97" for top and bottom borders

2 strips 2¼" x 88" for side borders

196 squares 1¾" x 1¾" for centers

WHITE:

2 strips 3¼" x 96" for top and bottom borders

2 strips 3¼" x 88" for side borders

(Cutting list continues on page 108)

Log Cabin

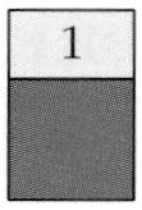

FIGURE 1. Sew strip (1) to side of center square.

FIGURE 2. Sew strip (2) to the pieced unit.

FIGURE 3. Sew strip (3), continuing the clockwise progression.

FIGURE 4. Sew strip (4), completing the first round of logs.

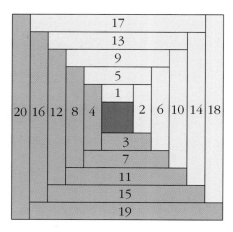

FIGURE 5. Continue to add logs in numerical order and a clockwise direction. Make 196 blocks that measure 6¼" before being sewn together.

(Cutting list continued)

✦ Cut 196 of each of the following log measurements, noting that the yardage is calculated for cutting strips across the width of the fabric that measure the length of the log, and then cutting the strips into 1"-wide logs.

PLACEMENT ORDER	SIZE
(1)	1" x 1¾"
(2)	1" x 2¼"
(5)	1" x 2¾"
(6)	1" x 3¼"
(9)	1" x 3¾"
(10)	1" x 4¼"
(13)	1" x 4¾"
(14)	1" x 5¼"
(17)	1" x 5¾"
(18)	1" x 6¼"

ASSORTED PRINTS:

✦ Cut 196 of each of the following log measurements.

PLACEMENT ORDER	SIZE
(3)	1" x 1¾"
(4)	1" x 2¼"
(7)	1" x 2¾"
(8)	1" x 3¼"
(11)	1" x 3¾"
(12)	1" x 4¼"
(15)	1" x 4¾"
(16)	1" x 5¼"
(19)	1" x 5¾"
(20)	1" x 6¼"

 VERTICAL QUILTS WITH STYLE – BOBBIE AUG & SHARON NEWMAN

SEWING DIRECTIONS

PIECING THE BLOCKS

Note: If a log is too short or too long, check the preceding seam. With logs cut to exact length, a ¼" seam is a must!

◆ Sew a (1) white strip to the side of a center red square. Press seam allowances away from the center square (Fig. 1).

◆ Add a (2) white strip to the pieced unit as shown. Press away from the center (Fig. 2).

◆ Sew a (3) print strip, continuing the clockwise progression. Each time, press away from the center (Fig. 3).

◆ Sew a (4) print log, completing the first round of logs (Fig. 4).

◆ Continue to add logs in numerical order and in a clockwise direction. Make 196 blocks (Fig. 5).

ASSEMBLING THE QUILT TOP

◆ Arrange four squares as shown in Figure 6. Sew 28 of this four-block unit.

◆ Arrange four squares as shown in Figure 7. Sew 21 of this four-block unit.

◆ Sew seven identical four-block units into a vertical row. Make four "zigzag" rows and three "cross" rows.

◆ Alternate the rows as shown in the quilt, matching seams.

ADDING THE BORDERS

◆ Sew the white and red side border strips together. Press allowances toward the red. Add the pieced borders to the sides of the quilt as described in Adding Borders with Straight Corners, page 16.

◆ Sew the white and red top and bottom border strips together. Press allowances toward the red. Add the pieced borders to the top and bottom of the quilt.

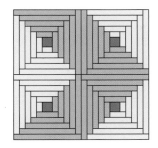

FIGURE 6. Arrange four squares as shown, sew 28 of this four-block unit.

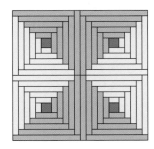

FIGURE 7. Arrange four squares as shown, sew 21 of this four-block unit.

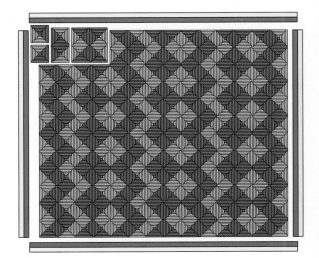

ASSEMBLY DIAGRAM

Log Cabin

FULL-SIZE QUILTING PATTERN

FINISHING THE QUILT

✦ Mark the quilting design. This quilt is quilted in the ditch by rows, creating concentric squares, with an "X" over the red center. A 2"-long single cable is quilted in the red border, with diagonal parallel lines ½" apart in the white borders.

✦ Layer quilt top, batting, and backing, and baste.

✦ Quilt and bind.

✦ Sign and date your quilt.

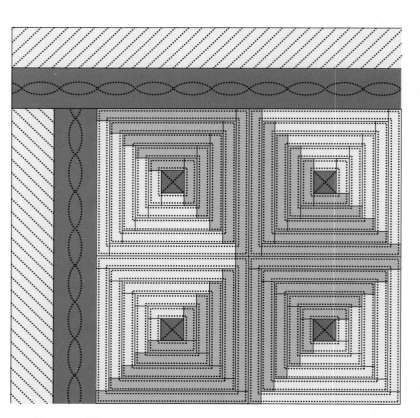

QUILTING DESIGN

About the Authors

Bobbie Aug and Sharon Newman met in Paducah, Kentucky, at the 1989 American Quilter's Society Show. Both were in the first group tested and certified as quilt appraisers by AQS. Currently, both serve as members of the AQS Appraiser Certification Program Committee. Sharon also serves as the program's administrator. Both learned to sew on treadle sewing machines, Bobbie in Illinois and Sharon in Indiana. Their love and appreciation of quilts brought them together, and they have been friends ever since. Together, the two have traveled to quilt shows, presented programs, judged quilt shows, taught classes, and appraised quilts.

Sharon's interest in quiltmaking began in Indiana as the granddaughter of a prolific quiltmaker. Since marrying her husband, Tom, and rearing three daughters, Tracy, Vicki, and Carol, Sharon has focused on quilts and quiltmaking with a well-known business, The Quilt Shop, and participation in the Texas Quilt Search. She has written seven books on quiltmaking and quilt history, and she is nationally recognized for her reproduction fabric lines from Moda Fabrics.

Bobbie Aug was inspired by the quiet, dignified beauty of nineteenth-century quilts and began making quilts 30 years ago. She became a quilt dealer, quilt collector, quilt shop owner, and quilt show consultant and producer, focusing on anything related to quilts and quiltmaking. Bobbie lives in Colorado Springs, Colorado, with her husband, Norm. Their family includes son Tony, daughter Carrie, Brittany spaniels Angel and Sadie, and a nasty cat named Phannie.

Bibliography

Marston, Gwen, and Joe Cunningham. *Sets and Borders*. Paducah, KY: American Quilter's Society, 1987.

Rae, Janet. *The Quilts of the British Isles*. New York: E. P. Dutton, 1987.

von Gwinner, Schnuppe. *History of the Patchwork Quilt*. West Chester, PA: Schiffer Publishing Ltd., 1988.

Other AQS Books

This is only a small selection of the books available from the American Quilter's Society. AQS books are known worldwide for timely topics, clear writing, beautiful color photos, and accurate illustrations and patterns. The following books are available from your local bookseller, quilt shop, or public library.

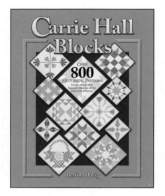

#4957 $34.95

#5211 $18.95

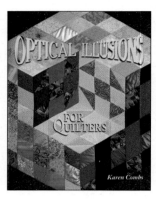

#4831 $22.95

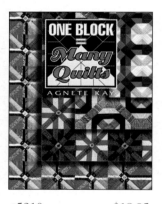

#5210 $18.95

#5710 $19.95

#4897 $19.95

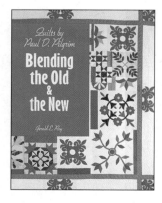

#4918 $16.95

#5339 $19.95

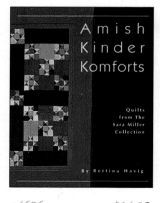

#4696 $14.95

LOOK FOR THESE BOOKS NATIONALLY OR CALL   **1-800-626-5420**